Wildlife and Wilderness
A History of Adirondack Mammals

Philip G. Terrie

Wildlife and Wilderness

A History of Adirondack Mammals

For Hildegard
Best wishes
Philip Terrie

PURPLE MOUNTAIN PRESS
Fleischmanns, New York

FIRST EDITION
1993

Published by
PURPLE MOUNTAIN PRESS, LTD.
Main Street, P.O. Box E3
Fleischmanns, New York 12430-0378

Copyright © 1993 by Philip G. Terrie

All rights reserved under International and
Pan-American Copyright Conventions.

Library of Congress Cataloging-in-Publication Data

Terrie, Philip G.
  Wildlife and wilderness : a history of Adirondack mammals / by Philip G. Terrie. -- 1st ed.
    p.   cm.
  Includes bibliographical references (p.   ) and index.
  ISBN 0-935796-38-X (hc : acid-free). -- ISBN 0-935796-39-8 (pbk.. : acid-free)
    1. Mammals--New York (State)--Adirondack Mountains--Ecology.
  2. Man--Influence on nature--New York (State)--Adirondack Mountains.
  3. Wildlife management--New York (State)--Adirondack Mountains--Moral and ethical aspects.   I. Title.
  QL719.N7T47   1993
  599.09747'5--dc20   93-4311
                                                                    CIP

Manufactured in the United States of America
Printed on acid-free paper

Cover and frontispiece:
Detail from James McDougal Hart, Untitled: Bit of Lake Placid, 1860.
Collection Adirondack Museum

Table of Contents

Preface
7
Introduction
"What Wild Animals Then Existed"
10
1 Native Americans and Adirondack Wildlife
23
2 Unicorns and Beaver
32
3 The John Cheney Era
46
4 Sportsmen and the Hunt
61
5 Murray's Fools
81
6 Limits and Seasons
96
7 Extirpation and Reintroduction
113
8 The Wildlife Bureaucracy
132
9 "The Hallmark of Quality"
147
Sources
163
Index
171

Preface

I FIRST CROSSED THE BLUE LINE, the boundary of the Adirondack Park, in June 1966, riding in a chartered bus. On a dark highway somewhere south of Long Lake we hit and killed a deer that leaped into our headlights. This was my first encounter with Adirondack wildlife. It was an experience rather less charming than a glimpse of a white-tail in a leafy glade or the sound of a beaver tail smacking the placid surface of an Adirondack pond. But it illustrated with dramatic finality how the story of the wildlife of this region is inevitably a story of animals *and* people. Understanding wildlife in the Adirondacks requires far more than a study of the details of population density, mortality, morbidity, availability of food, predation, parasites, and all the other non-human factors that affect numbers and diversity. It also involves what people have done to the animals and their range and what they have thought about the very idea of wild animals.

Since that night, I've seen many more deer (most of them alive and bounding away from me), an occasional bear, porcupine, raccoon, fisher, otter, mink, and beaver, and I've spotted uncountable small creatures like mice, chipmunks, squirrels, hares, and bats. Along the way, I've become intensely interested in all Adirondack mammals. I'm also interested in birds, reptiles, fish, spiders, insects, and all the other varied living things into whose space I periodically intrude, but this is a book about mammals.

Encounters with wildlife can be startling. One night on the Raquette River a few miles east of Tupper Lake, I woke up and found a gray fox standing on the foot of my sleeping bag. On another night, camping alone on Cold River, I was stirred from the sound sleep of a tired hiker by a bear cub chewing on the side of Seward lean-to. I've heard coyotes howling and yipping behind my camp on Long Lake. I'm quite certain that I saw a mountain lion cross the road in front of my car just east of Indian Lake. I'm still waiting to see a moose, which has become a mystical beast for me. I know they're there. I've talked to several people who have seen them. But for me they remain as elusive as the unicorn.

A major stimulus to my rudimentary understanding of Adirondack wildlife was a report written for the Adirondack Museum in 1972, the first version of this book. The museum was beginning to plan its exhibit "Woods and Waters" and hired me to prepare a report on wildlife. This much-revised version of that report is published with the permission of the Adirondack Museum. While I was writing that first draft, I was assisted almost daily by the librarian, Marcia Smith. During the lengthy period of rewriting, I have received much help from the current librarian, Jerold Pepper. Jim Meehan, Tracy Meehan, and Caroline Welsh were generous with their time when I was selecting illustrations.

After I left the museum in 1973, I put away my carbon copy of the report and nearly forgot all about it, though most of the primary documents I first read while writing it proved to be significant sources for my book *Forever Wild: Environmental Aesthetics and the Adirondack Forest Preserve*, published in 1985. I happened to mention the report to Barbara McMartin in 1983. She read through it and suggested that there might be a book there. After receiving editorial suggestions from her as well as from Jim Dawson and Fran Rosevear, I began rewriting. Subsequent drafts were read by Ted Comstock, Kenneth Kogut, and Al Schwartz. In addition to library research, I discussed technical aspects of the subject, either in person or through correspondence, with several wildlife experts. These included Greenleaf Chase, Donald Behrend, C. H. D. Clarke, George Davis, Peter Gaskin, C. W. Severinghaus, and Dale Garner. I am grateful to all who helped, even if I sometimes ignored or misunderstood what they told me. Only I, of course, am responsible for errors of fact or judgment that remain.

I should state here at the outset that I am not a hunter. I am not hostile to the idea of hunting; I just don't think I would personally enjoy it or be any good at it. I have no objection to people who want to get their own meat. As a meat-eater myself (and one who likes the taste of venison), it would be inconsistent for me to think otherwise. Hunting, I believe, is a sound and healthy way for an Adirondacker to feed his or her family and can be part of a quest for a deeper connection with nature. In his essay on "Wildlife in American Culture," Aldo Leopold, a hunter, put it well: "There is value in any experience that reminds us of our dependency on the soil-plant-animal food chain, and of the fundamental organization of the biota." But that is not to say that all hunters are necessarily searching for or achieve such an understanding.

PREFACE

Hunting is important to conservation. In the Adirondacks, the white-tailed deer, whose natural predators the wolf and mountain lion are no longer around, can overpopulate its range to the point of starvation. Hunting helps to keep the numbers of deer under control. Recreational hunting, moreover, has been part of the image of the Adirondacks for nearly a century and a half. Along with hiking, fishing, mountain climbing, skiing, and other sports, hunting is part of the romance and allure of the region.

During this century (but not necessarily in the last few years) the state conservation bureaucracy has promoted the deer population at the expense of other species. I believe that in the Adirondacks throughout most of this century state wildlife management goals have favored the needs of deer hunters while paying considerably less attention to the possibility of restoring the wildlife community that existed at the beginnings of white contact. Although hunting is but one form of recreation pursued in the Adirondacks, it preoccupied those charged with managing the Forest Preserve. Hunters have a way of claiming that their interests are consistently ignored. This is part of a defensive mentality that one encounters in virtually any magazine or book about hunting. I believe the record shows that, to the contrary, hunters have exercised considerable — one might say inordinate — influence on wildlife policy for the Adirondacks.

I have intentionally tried to keep this book from having the look and tone of a scholarly treatise. It is meant to be an entertaining and instructive but not pedantic study. Although the book is clearly a polemic, none of its arguments depend on the subtle use of evidence. I have therefore felt no need to maintain the apparatus of academic publishing. Instead of footnotes littering the text, I have provided a list of sources. Short portions of this book have appeared, in somewhat different form, in *Adirondack Life*, the *Journal of Sport History*, and the *Conservationist*.

This book is dedicated to the memory of two writers
who encouraged me to write:
Moncure F. Terrie and William K. Verner.

Introduction
"What Wild Animals Then Existed"

But to my notion, as the country grows old, it's an interestin' study to look into things as they were so long back, and see what wild animals, birds, fishes, and such things, then existed; to know what of them have been pushed entirely out of the world, and what of 'em have been left, and to understand what changes white men, and tame life all around 'em, have worked on 'em.

ADIRONDACK SPORTSMAN AND WRITER Samuel H. Hammond attributed these words to his guide, Tucker, in *Hills, Lakes, and Forest Streams* in 1854, at a time when the character of wildlife in the Adirondacks was in the midst of dramatic changes. The wolverine was probably gone, the moose had less than a decade left, the mountain lion and eastern timber wolf were threatened and would hold on tenuously only until the end of the century, and the white-tailed deer population was increasing. It would indeed have been an "interestin' study" in the mid-nineteenth century to examine these and other developments. And it is equally intriguing and important today when many people are committed to restoring the conditions whose loss Hammond was among the first to recognize.

The focus of this book is cultural and humanistic. That is, in addition to observing changes in circumstances and populations, I have attempted to trace the evolution of human attitudes toward the wild animals of the Adirondacks. How did people feel about the wild animals they trapped and

INTRODUCTION

shot? What did the wildlife mean to the Indians? the first whites? the modern Adirondack hunter? the urban or suburban backpacker? From our attitudes toward the animals we kill and those we save we can learn a great deal about what we think about ourselves and our world.

The character of wildlife in the Adirondacks is different today from what it was when white men first penetrated the region. Nor was the animal community at that time necessarily static or "balanced." Modern ecologists understand nature as a dynamic, constantly changing system — with or without human interference. Yet Euro-Americans have shown a remarkable proclivity for making nature's fluctuations or deviations from a balance much more severe. They have continually altered the environment to suit often temporary needs — sometimes intentionally, sometimes without understanding the consequences of their actions.

In *Changes in the Land* environmental historian William Cronon describes how the land, forests, waters, and animal populations of New England were altered between the time of first white settlement and the Civil War. In discussing these changes, he makes an important methodological point. He asks, how can we assess change without comparing one thing to another? In other words, are we assuming that nature existed in some sort of timeless equilibrium before Europeans began what was clearly a significant alteration of the New England environment?

To do so would be to insist that changes occur only as the result of human or, to be even more inaccurate, European activity. At the same time, Cronon asks further, are we assuming that this equilibrium, if it existed, was somehow qualitatively to be preferred in comparison with whatever succeeded it. If we are thinking along these lines, it may be because we are thinking of nature in what Cronon calls a "functionalist" mode. That is, we are thinking in terms of succession and climax. In this view, all the organisms of a given place tend toward a balanced climax condition. Once that climax is achieved, it perpetuates itself indefinitely. If we consider this conception of nature for a moment and do so in terms of the vast span of geological or even biological time, we can see that it ignores the imperatives of history by removing the environment from its own history. Neither natural nor human history is static. And nature and human history do not exist exclusive of each other. The point of this is that we should not assume that change in an environment is automatically a regrettable event, even that change effected by human activity. A chief characteristic of the environment is its dynamism.

On the other hand, I believe, it is perfectly reasonable to reach considered judgments on what condition we think best for a given environment at a given time and to manage it with specific goals in mind. Changes, however begun and promoted, may be arrested or, in some cases, reversed.

Sometimes they ought to be. One of the major goals of this book is to describe the conditions obtaining within the animal community of the Adirondacks in the early nineteenth century and to argue that restoring these conditions, to the extent possible, should be one aim of all those interested in the future of the Adirondacks.

This is not meant to be a doctrinaire diatribe against the Euro-American settlement of this continent. Changes have often seemed necessary, and it is pointless to criticize people of, say, the 1840s for not displaying the environmentally correct values of the 1990s. Nonetheless, some human actions have been short-sighted and arrogant, arising from ignorance or greed or both. Without belaboring too much the wisdom or stupidity of the changes worked on the Adirondack environment and its wild inhabitants, I shall try to observe those changes as they took place, from the time of the first white contact to the present.

Some of the motives for changing the character of wildlife in the Adirondacks — either directly or indirectly — were based on ignorance and fable. Some might appear odd to the modern empirical mind, such as the belief in the medicinal qualities of beaver testicles. Some were tragic, as the certainty that wolves and mountain lions, if left unchecked, would destroy both domestic stock and the Adirondack deer herd. As Madison Grant suggested in 1901 in an essay written for a New York State Forest, Fish, and Game Commission *Report*, the commonly shared understanding of wildlife or of any part of nature in any period is inevitably subjective and always liable to error: "The tales told by hunters and trappers around the campfire to-day show as fervid an imagination and as naive a disregard for the facts [as they did in the past]."

* * *

The French explorer, Jacques Cartier, on a crisp October day in 1535, was the first known European to see the Adirondacks. But his view from the top of a hill beside the St. Lawrence River (where an Indian village named Hochelaga occupied the site of the modern Montreal) was from such a distance that he could say little more than that there were indeed mountains far away to the south. A 1580 English translation of Cartier's account of his travels supplies this description of the view: "On the Northe side of it there are manye hilles to be seene, running Weaste and Easte, and *as many more on the South*" (my emphasis). The Native Americans with whom Cartier was trading and from whom he hoped to learn of a route to China may have known what the forest on those mountains was like, but if the Indians told him anything, he made no record of it.

INTRODUCTION

Our investigation of the history of Adirondack wildlife begins with some educated guesses about the nature of the forest on and surrounding those "hilles" that Cartier spotted off to the south. The species of trees in the Adirondacks today are roughly the same that were there back in the sixteenth century, long before the advent of lumbering, farming, and fires. But because Euro-Americans prized some species and ignored others, the relative proportion of each species in the arboreal community has changed. There is general agreement, moreover, that while various groups of Indians undoubtedly trapped, hunted, traveled, and lived seasonally here and there on the Adirondack plateau, no significant human-caused interference in the forest occurred before the arrival of whites in the late eighteenth and early nineteenth centuries.

Before white men came, as today, the largest tree in the Adirondack forest was the white pine — the conifer that one often sees towering fifty feet or more above the surrounding trees. It was the first tree sought by the loggers; before those first loggers started cutting, many white pines grew to a height of over a hundred and fifty feet. White pine thrives in sandy soil — of which there is an abundance in certain parts of the Adirondacks — and may have constituted a larger portion of the Adirondack forest than it now does. There are occasional stands of large white pine found today — the old-growth pines south of the Oswegatchie River, for example — but nothing like the ancient pines of pre-logging days. In 1609 Samuel de Champlain observed impressive stands of white pine along the shores of the lake that now bears his name. Eighty years later, a Major Winthrop described a portion of Washington County through which he was trying to lead a column of soldiers. He complained of "noe grass for horses," but marveled at the "exceeding tall white pine fit to mast any ship."

Over the last century and a half, loggers have harvested millions of board feet of Adirondack conifers. After the white pine, the red spruce and hemlock were cut, the former for lumber and the latter for its bark, which was used in tanning leather. The wood and brush were usually left to rot on the ground. Later, beginning around 1890, after the processes by which wood pulp could be converted to paper were perfected, loggers began to cut all softwoods for pulp. After this, size no longer mattered.

The softwoods were the money trees in the early days of lumbering, and the vast stands of hardwoods, which do not float well and were thus difficult to transport, were generally ignored. In the Adirondacks, as in the remainder of the state, hardwoods constituted a substantial portion of the forest. As Major Winthrop saw, of course, there were nearly pure stands of white pine at certain places. Conifers also dominated the high slopes of the mountains where spruce and balsam prevailed — and still do, since the higher up on a slope a tree is, the more dwarfed and therefore the less valuable it becomes as merchantable timber. But in the extensive areas of the Adirondacks between about one thousand and twenty-five hundred feet above sea level, northern hardwoods were common—particularly sugar maple, yellow birch, and American beech. In the field notes of Archibald Campbell, who surveyed the north line of the Totten and Crossfield Pur-

H. D. Turner, "Deer on St. Regis, at Night" (1883).
Collection Adirondack Museum

chase in 1772 and was possibly the first white man, certainly the first on record, to cross the central Adirondacks, the trees mentioned as markers are maples, tamarack, spruce, and many beech. He notes that the party traveled through vast stands of pure beech. Other common species would have included balsam fir, ash, aspen, white birch, and cherry.

The forest was thus a mixture of hardwoods and conifers, as today. But those trees were big: Ralph Waldo Emerson, writing of the virgin forest on Follensby Pond, where he camped in 1858, declared,

> Our patron pine was fifteen feet in girth,
> The maple eight, beneath its shapely tower.

INTRODUCTION

Because the conifers were cut so thoroughly over so long a period and because the hardwoods—less immediately useful, harder to transport—have been harvested more selectively and only relatively recently, the hardwoods, especially beech, are overrepresented in today's Adirondack forest.

The old-growth forest of the eighteenth century would have favored those species that do not require sunlight to generate new growth—in the Adirondacks, red spruce, eastern hemlock, balsam fir, sugar maple, and American beech. These shade-tolerant species are the Adirondack trees that can succeed themselves. Able to take root and grow in the shade, they constitute the climax species for this region. Other local species, like aspen, cherry, or white birch, require sunlight for new growth and thus appear only after a disturbance of some sort—fire, windfall, or logging, for example. Such localized disturbances must have occurred periodically, such as the tornado that touched down near Cranberry Lake in 1845 and carved a long swath known for years as the Great Windfall. Beaver damming would also have opened up certain areas to new growth. Local events like these would thus naturally have allowed those species needing sunlight to thrive for one generation.

But with the generally mature forest that undoubtedly covered most of the Adirondacks—known as a closed-canopy forest—there would have been very little sunlight penetrating to the forest floor and therefore a minimum of young trees growing where animals could reach them. Exceptions naturally existed, but the general character of the Adirondack forest during the summer was that of a dark, damp (because the thick humus of the forest floor, not directly warmed by the sun, would retain moisture much longer than the floor of an open, sunlit forest) region, strewn with fallen and decaying trees.

What animals inhabited that forest? First, there were probably fewer deer than there are today. Regardless of the condition of the forest, because of the severity and length of the winters, the Adirondacks do not provide optimum deer range. Deer will starve in the winter if deep snow inhibits their ability to move about. Before white men opened up the Adirondacks with lumbering and forest fires, there was relatively little for deer to eat: the staple of the white-tailed deer diet is the new growth of certain species of trees. Particularly in the winter, deer depend on white cedar, yellow birch, and red maple. Although these are all common in the Adirondacks, their availability in sufficient quantity in the winter and—what is most important—where deer could reach them would have been limited. In a closed canopy forest, new growth within reach would have been minimal.

In the winter, at the northern limit of the white-tail's range, as in the Adirondacks, deer "yard up," or concentrate on south-facing hillsides or in lowlands or other areas protected by conifers from the wind and snow. While this habit helps protect deer from severe weather and thus conserves energy, it leads to localized starvation in the yards where the browse is inadequate. Deer tend to return annually to the same yards. Wildlife managers have tried to drive deer from habitual wintering yards to unused areas where the browse is more plentiful, but these efforts generally fail. Although figures for the numbers of deer that actually starve during severe winters are impossible to establish with precision, some wildlife experts estimate that up to fifty percent of the fawns born the previous summer can die of malnutrition in a winter of low temperatures and deep snow. Such starvation, when it occurs in a place like the Adirondacks, reflects overpopulation of a marginal range.

Toward the end of the nineteenth century, the deer population grew larger in the increasingly open Adirondacks. Similar northward extensions of range have occurred across the continent, wherever forestry, fires, or agricultural practices offered new sources of browse. White-tailed deer experts William and RuthAnn Hesselton point out that these northward movements must be seen as "temporary in the sense that if these practices [forestry and agriculture] were ceased or were altered so that the habitat returned to primeval conditions, deer distribution would decline."

Ever since the late nineteenth century large numbers of deer have been maintaining a marginal existence in the Adirondacks, increasing beyond the capacity of the range whenever a number of mild winters follow in succession and starving in frightful numbers during winters of deep snows and intense cold. Since the earliest exploration and travel narratives mention deer, we can be certain that they lived in the Adirondacks before the arrival of white men, especially in areas where natural disturbances or beaver damming opened the canopy and permitted new growth, but the deer population then was smaller than it later became.

The other large hoofed animal, or ungulate, was the moose (elk did not inhabit the Adirondacks in historic times). Moose expert John W. Coady notes, "Moose are a species of the boreal forest. Their distribution is more closely related to the range of northern trees and shrubs than to any other factor. Moose eat a variety of plants, ranging from mosses to trees." The moose of North America thrive mostly in ranges on acid soil, and the soils of most of the Adirondack region are strongly acidic. Furthermore, the forest cover of the Adirondacks provides nearly all the items associated with the moose diet where it has been studied. These include, in the summer, sugar maple, mountain maple, mountain ash, white birch, yellow

INTRODUCTION

"Monarch of the Forest,"
Woods and Waters, 3 (1900).

birch, and aquatic plants, and, in the winter, balsam fir, maples, white birch, and aspen.

Moose are comfortable with snow, and unlike deer they can move around in deep snow with relative ease. In fact, they will gravitate to deeper snow for bedding, preferring a depth of around forty inches — a depth which almost completely inhibits the movement of white-tailed deer. In the summer the many natural ponds, beaver ponds, and wetlands in the Adirondacks would have provided an abundance of browse. In all, the Adirondacks of three centuries ago were much more suitable for moose than for deer, but there would not have been nearly as many moose then as there are deer now. For one thing, a moose eats about five to ten times more per day than a deer does. Areas in New Brunswick where deer and moose live near each other on the same type of (but not on the same) range support about 1.6 moose and about ten deer per square mile.

What about predators? The two largest carnivores were the eastern timber wolf and the mountain lion (the big cat also known as panther, painter, puma, or cougar). Studies of the wolf have shown that wolves prey on both white-tailed deer and moose, among other species. The moose, when healthy, is usually too formidable a target for a wolf or even a pack of wolves. Diseased, old, or very young moose, however, are often brought down by wolves. An Algonquin Park (Ontario) study showed that wolves supplemented their diet with beaver, hare, and other small animals, but deer composed the bulk of their food.

Although research on the mountain lion has not been as extensive as that on the wolf, the evidence points to a white-tailed deer diet for the Eastern great cat as well. The mountain lion, which occasionally weighs close to two hundred pounds, needs considerable protein to keep it active and healthy. While the mountain lion, like the wolf, will kill and eat smaller animals when the opportunity presents itself, it needs large prey, like deer.

Perhaps the largest population of mountain lions and wolves in the Adirondacks actually existed after the coming of the white man. As the deer herd grew in the central Adirondacks, predators might naturally have increased at the same time. This peak population, if it did indeed occur then, lasted for only a few decades. By 1871 there were state bounties on wolves and mountain lions; at the same time their natural habitat was being rapidly destroyed. Before the environmental changes of the nineteenth century these two large predators would have been few in number, but they would have served a useful purpose in limiting prey populations, especially of deer.

The third major predator (actually an omnivorous animal) was the black bear. As with most wild animals, population numbers are hard to

INTRODUCTION

estimate. Black bear expert Michael R. Pelton, observes, "Because of their generally sparse numbers, characteristic shy and secretive nature, and inaccessible habitat, black bears are difficult to census." For many years bears, like wolves and mountain lions, were thought of as pests, and bounties were paid on bears into the twentieth century. Pelton also notes that interaction between black bears and people can be troublesome: "Wherever the species exists, if allowed to do so, it has a tendency to adapt to the presence of people." In the Adirondacks and elsewhere this has led to a history of bears' becoming nuisances around cabins, popular campsites, and dumps. In the Adirondacks there are no animals bigger than the bear, and it has no natural enemies.

In addition to mountain lions, two other large cats—bobcats and lynx—inhabited the Adirondacks. These similar cats lived throughout much of North America, and they were trapped for fur soon after the first white men encountered them. Bobcats handled the pressures of hunting, trapping, and shrinking wild habitat much better than did lynx, and they are doing well throughout most of the United States. Lynx, on the other hand, steadily retreated before these pressures, and its United States range is now largely limited to a few remote places near the Canadian border. This includes the Adirondacks, where the lynx is a rare species, whose presence should be carefully guarded. Indeed, the Adirondack lynx may be extirpated. The Temporary Study Commission on the Future of the Adirondacks concluded in 1972 that although lynx appeared to be "scattered throughout the area," these represented strays. The Commission recommended granting complete protection to the lynx.

How many beaver were there? Population figures for the Adirondack beaver vary widely. In 1906 Harry Radford, well-known naturalist and writer, estimated that in 1600 there were one million beaver in the Adirondacks. This figure seems impossibly high in the light of current knowledge of the beaver's habits and needs. The Canadian biologist, C. H. D. Clarke, an expert on wildlife populations, studied the Adirondacks and compared the region with Ontario, with which it shares important topographical and environmental characteristics. On the basis of annual beaver harvest in Ontario and on his comparisons of the two areas, Clarke concluded that the Adirondacks could sustain a peak population of about 100,000 beaver. In any case, the many hundreds of miles of Adirondack brooks, flowing through terrain ideally suited for beaver-constructed impoundments, undoubtedly supported an extensive beaver population.

In addition to the beaver, several other animals prized for their pelts inhabited the Adirondacks. Among these are the otter, muskrat, mink, marten, fisher, and red and gray fox. The wolverine was extirpated soon after white men came into the region. Living along side these large and well-known mammals were assorted mice, moles, bats, voles, shrews, porcupines, raccoons, and rabbits. It is unfortunate that I cannot discuss the human impact on all the wildlife of the Adirondacks. For certainly, in the scheme of nature, to use an anthropomorphic expression, the rare pygmy shrew or the hoary bat is just as important as the moose, the wolf, or the economically significant white-tailed deer, and their histories are just as potentially interesting to the late twentieth-century reader. Regrettably, the primary literature on the wild animals of the Adirondacks, except within the last couple of decades, simply does not deal with the smaller species. In the entire nineteenth century only two writers, James DeKay and C. Hart Merriam, made any significant investigation into the Adirondack populations of smaller animals. Besides them there is virtually no mention of animals not valuable for their pelt or meat or intriguing for their putative ferocity.

This historical study of Adirondack wildlife depends on guidebooks, diaries of travelers and explorers, popular periodicals, and government reports. These documents were primarily concerned with the animals that possessed economic importance or made a picturesque impression on the traveler. People were interested in moose, deer, bear, wolves, mountain lions, and fur bearers. Because they are the animals described in the primary literature, they are the animals addressed, for the most part, in this book. The virtual absence of the smaller creatures from the literature of the last century indicates a preoccupation with the large and showy.

As far as the larger mammals are concerned, then, what Cartier might have seen if he had traveled to those southern mountains back in 1535 would have been a few moose, wolves, mountain lions, deer, beaver, and bear. The Adirondacks were not teeming with wildlife. The closed canopy of the forest would have limited the populations of the larger species. If we could walk through the Adirondacks of four centuries ago, we would be surprised by the scarcity of wildlife. Here and there one would see signs of an occasional animal, but most of all the impression would be of a vast, dark forest and an apparent absence of mammal life. The small animals would be all around but not constantly visible. The large animals would be seldom encountered. It would be a lonely hike through tangled matrices of fallen timber, nearly always in shadow, with little vegetation on the forest floor except for ferns and mosses. Most important would be the absence, near the ground, of young buds and shoots on the trees. Most of the new growth of those early Adirondack trees would have been at the top of the canopy, in the sunlight, and far out of the reach of any browsing deer or moose.

INTRODUCTION

Henry David Thoreau encountered such a forest in Maine in the middle of the nineteenth century and described it with his characteristic precision and wit:

> It was a mossy swamp, which required the long legs of a moose to traverse, and it is very likely that we scared some in our transit, though we saw none. It was ready to echo the growl of a bear, the howl of a wolf, or the scream of a panther; but when you fairly get into the middle of one of these grim forests, you are surprised to find that the larger inhabitants are not at home commonly, but have left only a puny red squirrel to bark at you.

Such a forest does not appeal to everyone, but those to whom wilderness is one measure of the aesthetic value of a forest would like to see large parts of the Adirondacks continue their return to this condition. The wildlife of a northeastern wilderness is subtle, various, and elusive. The fact that an unmanaged Adirondack wilderness does not support great herds of wildlife has been repeatedly advanced as an argument against keeping the Forest Preserve "forever wild," as the New York constitution stipulates. Such a view emphasizes quantity over quality, economics over history, and manipulation over the natural.

* * *

Several decades after Samuel Hammond's prescient observation about changes occurring in the Adirondack wildlife community, some New Yorkers, aware of the disappearance of certain animals, began to try to reintroduce these extirpated species. (Throughout this book, I use the term "extirpated" to describe local extinctions: i.e., in connection with an animal like the wolverine no longer found in the Adirondacks but still inhabiting at least part of its former range.) In any study of the attitudes toward and treatment of animals, the issue of reintroduction of extirpated species is a critical one. The people responsible for the failed attempt to stock the Adirondacks with elk, for example, believed they were performing a great service to the region and to nature, but we know now that the project could never have succeeded: the central Adirondack region is not good elk habitat. A project of stocking or restocking carries with it implications far beyond the simply aesthetic benefits of seeing rare or exotic animals in the woods. As it turned out, the elk all died (or were shot).

At the same time, moose were also restocked, and this effort also failed—to the dismay of everyone involved. A crucial reason for the failure may have been the presence of large numbers of white-tailed deer, which have become for many people the representative wildlife species in the Adirondacks. Deer commonly carry a nematode, or roundworm, *Parelaphostrongylus tenuis*, which in deer goes through an ordinary roundworm cycle and causes little harm but which in moose often results in a fatal brain illness, generally referred to as moose disease. Studies have shown that when white-tailed deer and moose inhabit the same range, some moose are infected by *P. tenuis*. This worm, according to wildlife experts, has the greatest impact on moose of any known disease or parasite and is the principal factor limiting the expansion of moose into new ranges or into old ranges from which it has been extirpated. And it may, at least partly, explain both the disappearance of moose from the Adirondacks during the mid-nineteenth century and the failure of that early restocking attempt.

The role of the white-tailed deer in the Adirondack forest is a controversial topic. The deer thrives in an environment that shows strongly the effects of human activity. While the moose, too, lives most comfortably in an environment affording various stages of succession (provided the deer population is under control), it is considerably more at home in an unmanaged forest than a deer is. The history of these two species, deer and moose, is thus one of the major topics of this book. It involves two equally intriguing animals, major changes in the Adirondack wildlife community, difficult questions about the future, and critical issues concerning wilderness and the human role in shaping the environment. These issues are at once biological, economic, aesthetic, and ethical. Deer and moose—both impressive, both fascinating to look at, both bearing a substantial burden of symbolism—constitute the spiritual and intellectual core of this book. I have much to say about other species, but these are the animals whose history structures the entire project.

1 Native Americans and Adirondack Wildlife

No EVIDENCE SUGGESTS THAT NATIVE AMERICANS inhabited the Adirondacks in large numbers or permanent settlements. To the north and south, the valleys of the St. Lawrence and Mohawk rivers would have provided a less severe climate and more abundant game. But hunting and war parties at one time or another ranged onto the Adirondack plateau, and on these excursions Indians undoubtedly became the first humans to have an impact on the local wildlife. By the sixteenth century, when Europeans were recording their early explorations of the terrain that would become New York, Ontario, and Quebec, we know that Native Americans were living and hunting all around the Adirondacks.

The Indians of those days kept no written records of their daily activities like hunting, but a few of the first white men to come into contact with them did. From their accounts we can glean some information about how the Indians lived, how they hunted, what they thought about the game they chased, and how the wildlife fit into their comprehension of their world. The environmental attitudes and ethics of these earliest Adirondack hunters were radically different from those of most of the white men who followed them.

We have no accounts of Indians actually hunting in the Adirondacks before the region was greatly changed by whites, but it seems logical that the Indians who lived all around the Adirondacks would have employed the same techniques wherever they hunted. The various species pursued outside the Adirondacks were nearly all found within what is now the Park, and we can assume that the way an Indian hunted deer in Ontario or along the Hudson would be the same as in the Adirondacks.

WILDLIFE AND WILDERNESS

Samuel de Champlain's description of a hunt on the shore of Lake Ontario supplies one of the first descriptions of a major Indian practice, the drive :

> Stags and bears are here very abundant. We tried the hunt and captured a large number as we journeyed down. It was done in this way. They place four or five hundred savages in line in the woods, so that they extend to certain points on the river; then marching in order with bow and arrow in hand, shouting and making a great noise in order to frighten the beasts, they continue to advance until they come to the end of the point. Then all the animals between the point and the hunters are forced to throw themselves into the water, as many at least as do not fall by the arrows shot at them by the hunters. Meanwhile the savages, who are expressly arranged and posted in their canoes along the shore, easily approach the stags and other animals, tired out and greatly frightened in the chase, when they readily kill them with the spear-heads attached to the extremity of a piece of wood of the shape of the half-pike.

Champlain's rendition of an Indian deer drive,
Voyages et Descourvertures (1618).

This hunt employed methods later used by white hunters in the Adirondacks. Various improvements were added, but the principle remained the same. Drive deer into the water, with either men or dogs, and kill them from small boats.

The white-tailed deer was a major part of the diet of the eastern Indians, and driving appears to have been one of the most efficient hunting techniques, employed whenever large quantities of venison were needed and enough men were available to participate in a drive. In another hunt described by Champlain, the Indians, before the drive, constructed a triangular palisade, open on one side. The two walls of the structure were fifteen hundred paces long and eight or nine feet high. At the closed end the Indians built an impoundment with an opening about five feet wide. The entire structure took them ten days to assemble. When the enclosure was completed, the Indians spread out into the woods about a mile from the open end and drove deer toward it by beating sticks together and slowly moving forward. The deer were forced by the steadily closing sides of the triangle to enter the smaller enclosure at the apex, while the Indians hastened them along by howling and barking like wolves. Once inside the small impoundment, the deer were killed with bows and arrows. In the late seventeenth century, Baron LaHontan, a French nobleman, witnessed a deer drive into a similar enclosure. When the drive was nearing completion and the slaughter was about to begin, the Indians allowed all the does to escape.

David DeVries, a Dutchman, described a drive near the Hudson in about 1642. As with the hunt described by Champlain where deer were driven to water, the Indians shot as many as possible with arrows before the deer reached the river. Indians in canoes waited for the rest. In the hunt described by DeVries, moreover, the Indians employed another technique that found its way into the repertoire of white Adirondack hunters:

> When the animals swim into the river, the savages lie in their canoes with lassos, which they throw around their necks, and tighten, whereupon the deer lie down and float with the rump upwards, as they cannot draw breath.

In the Adirondacks the lasso would become a slim sapling (often of birch) with a loop on the end. Sometimes a deer driven to water would be seized by the tail or even, as is related in one case on the St. Lawrence, the ear. When an Indian had grabbed the animal, he dragged it to shallow water where he could finish it off with a knife.

When the numbers of either men or game were not large enough for driving, Indians still-hunted or stalked. This involved finding individual

WILDLIFE AND WILDERNESS

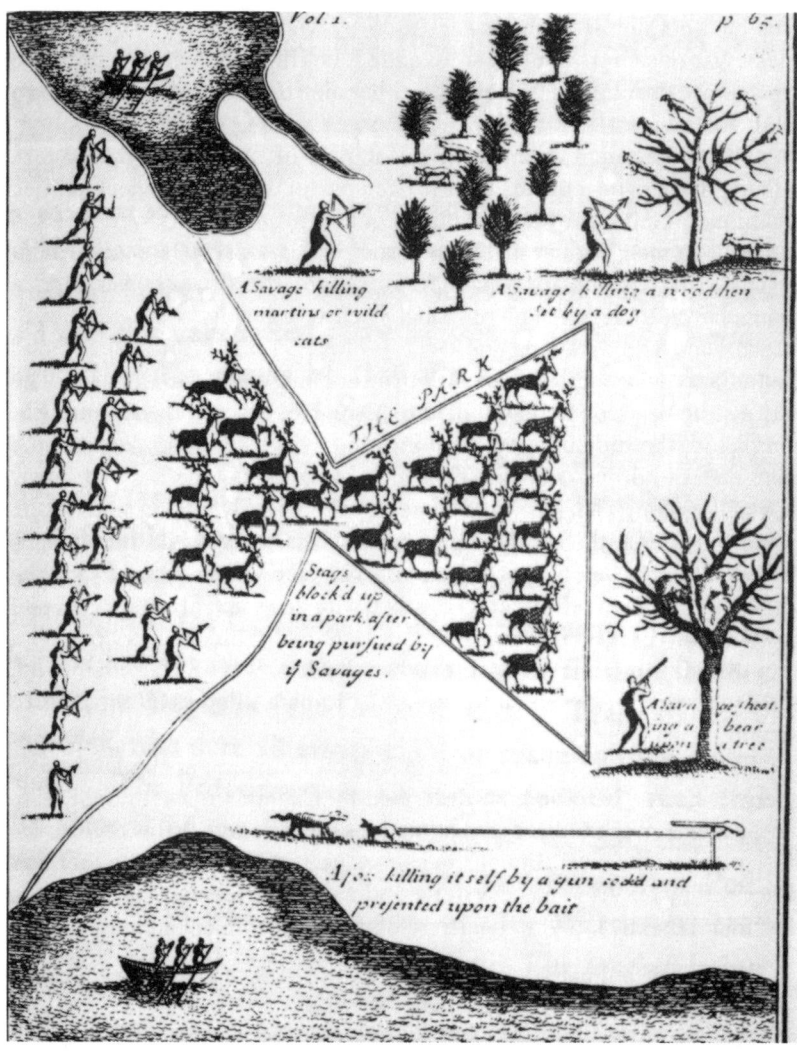

LaHontan, "The Hunting of divers Animals,"
New Voyages to North America (1703).

animals in the forest and shooting them on the spot, if possible, or chasing them. Often the first step in still-hunting was the discovery of tracks. In attempts to bring the deer in close, some hunters would lure them with salt or imitate the bleating of a fawn. Those who stalked deer often dressed themselves in deerskin. Another variation of still-hunting was for the hunter to station himself in a tree above a known deer path or runway.

Snowshoes would have been particularly useful where deep snow is common. In the Adirondacks the snow is occasionally so deep as to inhibit the movements of even a moose, and in the early spring the snow often has a hard crust. While the sharp-hoofed moose or deer breaks through with every step, a human hunter on snowshoes is especially mobile. At times like this the Indian could approach a moose close enough to kill it with a spear. LaHontan accompanied a group of Algonquins on a winter moose hunt in Canada and was greatly impressed with the efficiency of the Indians' snowshoes. After the Indians and LaHontan had constructed bark huts for shelter, several Indians went out as scouts to search for moose tracks in the snow. As soon as tracks were discovered, the rest of the party was sent for, so "The whole Company might have the pleasure of seeing the chase." LaHontan observed that the condition of the snow was a very important factor. If there was a crust, the moose were able to move only a short distance before the Indians overtook and killed them. But if the snow was soft or freshly fallen, a long chase could result unless the Indians' dogs were able to stop the moose in particularly deep snow. On LaHontan's hunt fifty-six moose were taken. The Indians, not inclined to kill more game than they needed, could have killed twice that number.

Bow, spears, and knives were not the Indian's only weapons. Baron LaHontan described a porcupine taken near the outlet of Lake Champlain in 1687. After it was treed by dogs, the Indians felled the tree with axes and then killed the porcupine from a distance with stones. Hunting muskrats in the same area, the Indians with LaHontan waited at dawn around the muskrat holes. When the animals emerged, the Indians plugged the holes and set their dogs on the muskrats. These same dogs also attacked a wolverine.

The Indians of New York often burned over a forested area and kept it clear with subsequent fires to sustain a source of deer browse and areas where deer would be easily hunted. Adriaen Van der Donck remarked on this practice in 1655 in his *A Description of New Netherlands*:

> The Indians have a yearly custom (which some of our Christians have also adopted) of burning the woods, plains and meadows in the fall of the year.... First, to render hunting easier, as the bush and vegetable growth renders the walking difficult for the hunter, and the crackling of the dry substances betrays him and frightens away the game.... Thirdly, to circumscribe and enclose the game within the lines of the fire.

Timothy Dwight, president of Yale College, who traveled in eastern New York and reached the southeastern Adirondacks early in the nineteenth century, remarked that the local Indians had annually burned over dry areas to prevent the forest from reclaiming what once had been timbered land and to "produce fresh and sweet pasture for the purpose of alluring deer to the spots on which [the fires] had been kindled."

Such burning promoted an "edge environment," areas of scrub and brush characteristic of the boundary between forest and meadow. This type of habitat is ideal for a great variety of wildlife species, especially deer, but also hares, grouse, and other useful food animals. When Indians benefited from the species promoted by these burned areas, writes William Cronon, "they were harvesting a foodstuff which they had been consciously instrumental in creating." A further benefit of burning has been demonstrated by modern research. Studies made in the Adirondacks and elsewhere have shown that deer prefer the browse on areas that have been burned: the protein content and the level of phosphorus and other trace minerals on a burn average somewhat higher than that of plants on unburned soil.

In the Adirondacks two areas which have been most often suggested as having been the locations of Indian burns are the plains of the Moose and Oswegatchie rivers. Indians living in either the St. Lawrence or Mohawk Valleys may well have entered the Black River Valley in search of game and moved up the Moose River. Both the Moose and the Oswegatchie offer ideal areas for burning since the plains would have been attractive to deer in the winter and would have facilitated clear shots with their open spaces. Although this seems logical, these areas may have arrived at their plains condition through strictly natural processes.

* * *

The most important feature of Indian hunting is the spirit in which it was conducted. In recent years, historians writing on the relationship between the Northeastern Indians and their environment (notably Calvin Martin, Neal Salisbury, and William Cronon) have added immeasurably to our knowledge and understanding of Indian ways — although these scholars do not necessarily agree with one another in their conclusions. Survival for the Indians demanded an intimate awareness of natural processes and phenomena, best illustrated, perhaps, in the woodcraft needed for a successful winter hunt. The Indian diet exploited a host of plant and animal species, and tribes or families of Indians ranged throughout their environment, harvesting their food according to a profound, almost intuitive understanding of seasonal, topographical, and biological details.

All the early European narratives suggest, moreover, that the Indians, though they manipulated their environment with great skill (as with agriculture or fires), exercised relatively little impact on it. The Indian population itself, through mechanisms not now completely understood, remained stable. This in turn assured a stability in the relationship between the Indians and the environment that sustained them. The Northeastern environment was managed efficiently and benignly by its Native American inhabitants.

Once game was killed, nothing was wasted. Hides became clothing, moccasins, and shelter. Bones became tools, ornaments, and weapons. All the edible portions were consumed, either by the Indians or their dogs. This included grease, which was boiled out of the carcass and drunk pure or used as butter, and marrow, which was extracted from crushed bones and eaten. After the hunt into the palisade, Champlain observed that the Indians "made good use of" the 120 deer killed, "reserving the fat for winter, which they use as we do butter." In short (and obviously), hunting was not a form of recreation. It was an activity necessary to the survival of both individuals and the tribe.

Probably because of the vital necessity of hunting, Indians displayed feelings about the animals they killed that were different from ours. The Indian hunter felt that he was a part of an animate landscape. All the creatures of that landscape — both human and nonhuman — enjoyed equal status. Indian folklore generally bestowed what we would call human characteristics on animals, birds, and fish. The Northeastern Indians believed that animals essential to the well-being of the tribe in effect allowed themselves to be killed because of the spiritual affinities among all creatures. Other animals were thought to assist their Indian brothers in the vital activities of the hunt. Baron LaHontan described a mountain lion that, the Indians persuaded him, helped them in their hunting. "The Savages call these Animals a sort of *Manitous*, that is, Spirits that love Men; and 'tis upon that score they esteem and respect 'em to such a degree, that they would choose rather to die, than to kill one of 'em." The Indian hunter respected all the animals around him and invoked a host of ceremonies and rituals to propitiate their spirits. If these rituals were overlooked or improperly pursued, the animals might withhold their bounty or cooperation.

This picture of Indian hunting and attitudes toward wildlife may seem idealized, the product of a twentieth-century consciousness imagining a response to nature preferable to western rapaciousness. Surely, one might claim, the Indians would have killed more game and perhaps wasted it if they had only possessed the technology, the guns and other modern devices introduced by Europeans. In *Keepers of the Game: Indian-Animal Relationships and the Fur Trade,* historian Calvin Martin demolishes the argument that Indian attitudes toward game were just as exploitative as the European ones that replaced them and that Indians simply lacked efficient technology. Martin demonstrates that the Indians were intuitively aware that their survival and well-being depended on a stable food supply. This implicitly understood dependence resulted in an Indian reverence for nature acknowledging the role of wildlife in supporting Indian existence. While such an awareness has been clearly demonstrated in the ethos of many so-called "primitive" peoples, it seems conspicuously absent in most of the relations between Euro-Americans and the environment that likewise sustains them but whose essential role has too often been ignored.

As historians of Indian attitudes and values have shown, Indians lived comfortably in an environment they altered to suit their needs but whose capacity to support them was not disturbed. Nature, in other words, was something familiar, benign, and close. Indeed, most Indians saw themselves as part of nature, as no more or less significant than deer, moose, or beaver. The important point is the notion of a culture's perceiving itself to be *in* nature, related to it, deeply involved in both physical and spiritual ways. This is the implication of Indian stories—creation myths, for example— wherein animals like beaver or wolves are referred to in anthropomorphic terms as the Indians' brothers and sisters.

There is at least one important alternative to this view of Indian attitudes to nature. The view described above, emphasizing the intuitive, animistic involvement of Indians in nature, I call the spiritual interpretation. It holds that Indians perceived inherent truths in nature that western civilization long ago forgot. One of the best examples of this interpretation is Calvin Martin's *Keepers of the Game,* a brilliant and moving analysis of Indian-animal interaction and of how the primal harmony between Indians and the game species on which their culture and survival depended was utterly disrupted by Europeans.

The other view, which I call materialistic, gets its most succinct treatment in William Cronon's *Changes in the Land: Indians, Colonists, and the Ecology of New England.* Cronon's interpretation of the relationship between Indians and the New England wilderness before white contact emphasizes modes of production rather than spirituality. In both views, the Indians took good care of the environment, but (to reduce often subtle distinctions to a crude level) Cronon, who cites Marx and Engels at the outset, sees the explanation for this solely in the Indians' sense of efficient and wise use of resources, while Martin invokes an image of a non-western people living in an animate, mystical world, where all living creatures shared spiritual bonds. In either case, the Northeastern Indians, before the arrival of Europeans, neither hunted a species to the point of extinction nor altered the environment to the extent that it could no longer support animals that once thrived there.

2 Unicorns and Beaver

TO THE FIRST EUROPEAN SETTLERS the vast, forested wilderness of the Northeast must have seemed awesome and mysterious. Coming from a largely cultivated and familiar Old World, confronting a seemingly endless forest, those early Dutch, British, and French (the Europeans most likely to get near the Adirondacks, and hence the ones with whom we are concerned here) knew little about either the people or the animals inhabiting North America. Prepared to believe almost anything about their new home, European settlers peered into the forest with apprehension and uncertainty. William Bradford, first Governor of Plymouth Plantation in Massachusetts, described in revealing terms his frightened little band's initial response to the New World: "Besides, what could they see but a hideous & desolate wilderness, full of wild beasts & wild men — and what multitudes there might be of them they knew not?"

Not knowing just what "wild beasts" lurked in the wilderness led to tales of fabulous and mythical creatures. Probably, the Indians learned early in the course of their contact with whites that some white men would believe anything, and Indian story tellers were apparently not reluctant to feed an appetite for fantastic tales. These passed into histories and other descriptive literature and appeared to confirm the strange nature of the New World wilderness. The Dutch chronicler Arnoldus Montanus, for example, depicted a veritable menagerie of weird animals that he said inhabited New Netherlands. Of the local eagles he wrote:

> They are excessively lascivious, so that they go together more than thirty times a day, not only with their own kind, but even with the female hawks and she wolves. They hatch out the large eggs in thirty, and the small in twenty days. They usually breed two to three young, whose eyes they turn towards the sun's rays. If these regard

the light of heaven without blinking they bring them up, otherwise, those that cannot stand such a test are driven from the nest. The young, as soon as they begin to fly, are taken up into the air and, left there to themselves, are sustained by the old birds. . . . Their breath stinks badly, wherefore the carcasses on which they feed rot rapidly, and though lascivious they are long lived: they die mostly of hunger, as the bill becomes by age so crooked that they cannot open any thing. Whereupon they finally fly to the highest regions toward the sun, tumble down into the coldest stream; they pluck out their feathers, clammy with sweat, and thus breathe their last.

Adriaen Van der Donck was told by Indians that in the northern woods were pure white deer as well as some perfectly black. "The savages say that the white deer are of very great consequence in the estimation of the other deer, and are exceedingly beloved, regarded and honored by the others, but that the reverse is true of the black deer." It is interesting to note that albinism is occasionally reported among deer in the Adirondacks today, but melanism is extremely rare.

Samuel de Champlain reported an enormous fish, perhaps a sturgeon, which the Indians caught in Lake Champlain. According to the Indians, who called the fish *Chaeusarou*, it was often ten feet long and captured birds by lying in shallow water like a log; an unsuspecting bird landing on it was pulled under water and drowned. The Indians used the teeth of this huge fish to treat headaches, scratching themselves where the pain was most severe. Claims that parts of the wild animals of the New World could alleviate pain or disease were common. Writing about the moose, which he said would die from the slightest wound and was often afflicted with epilepsy (he may have been describing the effects of the brain disease), Montanus declared that "the hooves cure the falling sickness." He further insisted that "when hunted they spew out hot water on the dogs."

It is not surprising that a large body of folklore should revolve around the beaver — the animal almost solely responsible for the existence of both the first Dutch trading posts along the Hudson and those of the French on the St. Lawrence. Some of the mythology associated with the beaver was imported from Europe, where for thousands of years people had believed that castoreum, or castor, an oily substance contained in two sacs between the anus and external genitals of both male and female beaver, was a cure for, among other things, colic, rheumatism, arthritis, and pleurisy. Not only does castor have no known medicinal value, but up until around the seventeenth century it was inaccurately thought to be produced by the male beaver's testicles.

Baron LaHontan insisted that castor did not come from the testicles and corrected the commonly held belief, first popularized in the *Natural History* of Pliny the Elder, that the male beaver, when chased, would bite off his testicles and leave them behind to escape with his life. LaHontan chastised later writers for promulgating this notion. He did declare, however, that beaver are one hundred times as intelligent as some people. Montanus also berated the ancients for believing that beavers castrated themselves but added to the list of maladies cured by castor: "mania, retention of the afterbirth, amenorrhoea, dizziness, gout, lameness, belly and tooth aches, dullness of vision, and poisoning." He credited beaver with building houses five stories tall, as did Van der Donck.

Montanus's description of the black bear was equally fantastic. According to Montanus, a shot bear will dress his wound with leaves and chase the hunter. If the man climbs a tree, the bear will climb above him lock his legs around the man's head, and jump out of the tree. When bears hibernate, wrote Montanus, they sleep on one side, growling continuously and sucking on a paw. After six weeks, the bear turns over and sleeps for six more weeks. Van der Donck included the same story and was probably the source for Montanus.

The most exotic of all the creatures described by Van der Donck and Montanus, however, was one that students of European mythical beasts will recognize. According to Van der Donck, who assured readers that his information came to him on the strictest authority from certain Mohawks,

> Far in the interior parts of the country, there were animals which were seldom seen, of the size and form of horses, with cloven hoofs, having one horn in the forehead, from a foot and a half to two feet in length, and that because of their fleetness and strength they were seldom caught or ensnared.

Montanus' description of this peculiar animal was more complete:

> On the borders of Canada animals are now and again seen, somewhat resembling a horse; they have cloven hoofs, shaggy manes, a horn right out of the forehead, a tail like that of the wild hog, black eyes, a stag's neck & love the gloomiest wildernesses; are shy of each other so that the male never feeds with the female except when they associate for the purposes of increase. Then they lay aside their ferocity; as soon as the rutting season is past, they again not only become wild, but even attack their own.

The unicorn had been a part of European mythology for two thousand years, appearing first in the fifth century B.C. in the works of Ctesias, a Greek living in Persia. Throughout the succeeding centuries, tales of miraculous powers attributed to the unicorn's horn circulated among European scholars and in the popular culture, and ostensible pieces of the horn sold for huge sums. Thus it comes as no surprise that Europeans in the New World, who were always eager to believe that they were on the verge of discovering sources of great wealth, should convince themselves that unicorns thrived in the unexplored interior.

"Wild Animals of New Netherland," from "Description of New Netherland, 1671" by Arnoldus Montanus, *The Documentary History of the State of New York* (vol. 4, 1851).

One explanation for these stories of unicorns in New York is that someone encountered a moose or deer with only one horn, and as the incident was told and retold, the animal became a unicorn. Deer have been reported with spike horns growing out of the middle of the forehead. Another possibility is the narwhal, an unusual animal itself, having one spiralled tusk extending nine or ten feet straight out from its mouth. In Europe narwhal tusks had been passed off as unicorn horns since the early Middle Ages. Perhaps a narwhal, which ordinarily inhabits arctic waters, died somewhere along the St. Lawrence, and its flesh rotted away. Whatever the case, at least two writers believed that unicorns inhabited the wild forests of New Netherlands, and Montanus placed the animal close to, if not in, the Adirondacks.

That such a beast loved the "gloomiest wildernesses" suggests what the wilderness signified when it started just the other side of the fence and stretched away for thousands of miles. No one knew what really existed in those forests, and there was no reason to doubt any claims; anything was possible. In an age when new peoples and animals were being discovered all around the world, the existence of a unicorn in the Adirondacks probably seemed just as likely as the existence of apes bigger than humans.

The popularity of fabulous stories about wildlife is a function of cultural values and attitudes. In his excellent study of wolves—both real and imaginary—Barry Lopez notes the persistence of folklore about wolves, appearing first in ancient myths and remaining common through the beginning of the Enlightenment in the early eighteenth century. These fanciful stories were most common in medieval bestiaries, compilations of lore and belief about various animals. Lopez finds tales about wolves that eat mud and wolves capable of blinding a man by looking at him as well as anecdotes about the curative powers of wolf hair. Such bits of folklore circulated in the pre-modern era and were similar to the tales of mythical animals in the forests of New York. The writers who purveyed these tales did so just as the western mind was emerging from the last grip of the Middle Ages. The belief in unicorns and lascivious eagles represented a vestige of the medieval mind.

* * *

A more pervasive and perhaps more troubling burden of western culture was its absolute faith in the idea that animals were created by God solely to be exploited by humans. In contrast to the Indians who first hunted and trapped in the Adirondack region, the Europeans who followed them were exponents of a radically anthropocentric mentality. The Indians saw animals and humans as equally significant creatures, sharing the earth, cooperating with one another in the perpetuation of sacred life forces.

The historian Lynn White, Jr., in a 1967 essay ("The Historical Roots of Our Ecological Crisis") that has become a central and controversial document in the study of western attitudes towards all of nature, argued that the chief villain in the western abuse of nature was Christianity itself. The Judaeo-Christian tradition, asserted White, is "the most anthropocentric religion the world has seen." The first Europeans in the new world, like their American descendents, represented a culture that has often viewed nature in an hierarchical, unequal way. God's words to Adam in the Book of Genesis supply perhaps the earliest and certainly one of the most succinct expressions of this tradition:

> Then God said, "Let us make man in our image, after our likeness; and let them have dominion over the fish of the sea, and over the birds of the air, and over the cattle, and over the earth, and over every creeping thing that creeps upon the earth." So God created man in his own image, in the image of God he created him; male and female he created them. And God blessed them, and God said to them, "Be fruitful and multiply, and fill the earth and subdue it; and have dominion over the fish of the sea and over the birds of the air and over every living thing that moves upon the earth."

In this passage from one of the fundamental documents of western civilization, we can see at least two significant features of the western attitude toward wildlife. First, only humans are created in God's image, and hence only they enjoy special status when compared to other species. The God of Genesis blesses the humans; he does not bless his other animate creations. Second, the humans are explicitly given dominion over all other living things. Ordered by God to "subdue" the earth, Adam and Eve are further instructed to exercise authority over the animals of air, water, and earth. White's point is not that Christianity is directly responsible for environmental abuses or that it instructs people to degrade nature. Rather, Christianity promulgated a set of values that appeared to promote anthropocentrism.

Throughout the history of western civilization the implications of this world view have manifested themselves with often disastrous consequenes. Humans reared in the Judaeo-Christian tradition have consistently acted as if they were superior to all living things. Believing that only they contained anything divine or sacred, they have viewed animals as soul-less, often profane, certainly expendable creatures. Of course, a dissenting view, illustrated by a thinker like St. Francis of Assisi, for example, has existed along side the majority position, but it has seldom displayed much force in our culture. In recent years, it seems to have attracted more and more people, however, as many Americans and others have begun to question the mainstream attitude, suggesting that the Indian view of nature as suffused with spirit and equality may be an improvement on our anthropocentric stance.

Since Lynn White first published his article criticizing the anthropocentrism of the Judaeo-Christian attitude toward nature, it must be noted, a number of other historians have pointed out inconsistencies and flaws in his position. The pre-Christian Romans, they observe, did a much better job of subjugating and controlling the natural world than did the Medieval Christians. Other non-Christian peoples have abused their resources and polluted their air and water; the Japanese affection for nature has not prevented frightful environmental problems in recent years. The same could be said of many other non-Christian countries. White's opponents argue that capitalism and industrialism, combined with uncontrolled population growth, not the intellectual, spiritual framework of Christianity, explain the degradation of nature found all around the world.

But to say that other religious traditions have not prevented environmental degradation does not contradict the discovery of a deep, essential anthropocentrism in the western mind. It is useless to lay all the blame for western environmental problems at the feet of Judaeo-Christianity, but it is impossible to deny that the capitalistic, industrial conception of nature, with its consistent disregard for the intrinsic value of animals, matured in a Christian Europe and now dominates the world. While God's instructions to Adam alone by no means account for all the environmental abuses that followed, they certainly made it easier for western man to commit them.

The pervasive assumption that it was correct and providentially destined for humans to dominate nature underlay and subtly justified the more overt economic and exploitative motives of the first white men to encounter Adirondack wildlife. The typical European settler of the New World shared the values of this fragment of eighteenth-century English verse:

> The brute creation are his property,
> Subservient to his will, and for him made.

And in the vast forests of the New World, European entrepreneurs saw enormous and hitherto untapped populations of wildlife. In terms of overt motives, neither colonization nor religion opened up this part of North America: it was the dream of accumulating quick fortunes trafficking in the pelts of wild animals, chiefly beaver, some of which lived in the Adirondacks.

* * *

The importance of the fur trade to Europe can hardly be overstated. The wearing and ownership of furs, which before the discovery of America were produced in every country in Europe, had acquired a nearly mystical significance. An English chronicler named Charrier declared,

> For the use of furs cures headach[e] and stomach ache; rheumatism, which defeats the most powerful remedies, is

removed by the skins of cats, of lambs, and of hares.... Of all the ornaments which luxury has invented there are none so glorious, so august, and so precious as furs.

So great, in fact, was the European demand for furs of all kinds that by the fifteenth century the catch of native fur bearers was no longer sufficient to meet the needs of the countries of Western Europe. For a while Russia and the rest of Eastern Europe supplied the furs required by the West, but eventually changing styles and economic and political factors had forced many western nations to protect their nascent textile industries with tariffs and other restrictions designed to keep Russian furs off the market. But the people still demanded furs, and each country in Western Europe sought some new supply. It was only logical that the eyes of speculators and investors should turn to the forests of America. France began trading for furs along the St. Lawrence, Britain in New England and Virginia, the Netherlands along the Hudson and Mohawk rivers, and Sweden along the Delaware.

One of the earliest incidents of fur trading between Indians and white explorers occurred on Cartier's first voyage—a year before he ascended Mont Royal. In certain ways it is typical of the later fur trade as well as of the subsequent relationship between white men and Indians:

> two of our men ventured to go on lande to them [the Indians], and carrie them knives wyth other Iron wares, and a red hat to give unto their Captain. Which when they saw, they also came on land, and broughte some of their skinnes, and so began to deale with us, seeming to be very glad to have our iron wares.... They gave us whatsoever they had, not keeping anything, that they were constrained to go backe againe naked.

To say that the Indians gave the white men the very shirts off their backs is no exaggeration.

This minor trade initiated by Cartier preceded the real onset of fur trading by about sixty-five years. It was not until around 1600 that enough capital was available for investors to spur serious trade in American pelts. This availability of capital was coupled with an increased popularity of furs. Beaver hats were in great demand, and fur linings and trim became fashionable. French speculators remembered the voyages of Cartier, and various attempts were made to establish trading colonies along the St. Lawrence, first at Quebec and later at Lachine.

By 1604 Samuel de Champlain was involved with the French trade, and under his guidance it grew, with occasional setbacks, into a profitable enterprise, although the complaints of other French merchants and sailors eventually caused Champlain's company to lose its monopoly. The extensive trade in the early part of the seventeenth century quickly opened up avenues to the even more plentiful sources of fur around Hudson Bay and the Great Lakes. The demand for furs was voracious: Champlain himself reported an incident wherein French traders removed the beaver robes from the bloody corpses of Iroquois warriors slain by Champlain and his Algonquin allies near the mouth of the Richelieu River in 1610.

At about the same time that the French were trading with the Algonquins along the St. Lawrence, the Dutch were making overtures to the Iroquois tribes in what became New York. In 1609 Henry Hudson, an Englishman sailing under Dutch colors and searching for a water route to the Orient, discovered the river now named after him and explored it as far north as the confluence with the Mohawk, where he met Indians, several of whom came aboard: "And many brought us Bevers skinnes, and Otters skinnes, which wee bought for Beades, Knives, and Hatchets." The next day Hudson got several Indians drunk, thus establishing another precedent in white-red relations.

After Hudson returned to Amsterdam with tales of the rich quantities of furs in the New World, Dutch merchants, watching foreign furs flood their market and weary of paying the high prices demanded by the French and Russians, were quick to see the potential for profits in a North American fur trade. They soon set up their own companies to trade in furs that had not passed through French hands. The year after Hudson's first voyage other Dutch ships returned to the land of the Iroquois and established an alliance with them based on the fur trade. The Iroquois were already at war with the Algonquin allies of the French, and a struggle for fur resources became part of the conflict. Since the Adirondacks lay between the traditional territories of these two Indian groups, Adirondack furs probably contributed to both the French and Dutch trade, sent to Montreal by Algonquin trappers and to New Amsterdam by Iroquois.

By 1621 the Dutch West India Company was granted a charter by the States-General of the Netherlands, and despite the fact that the English claimed the Hudson, the Dutch went ahead with full-scale trading. In a very few years they were making huge profits, and one contemporary writer observed, "Rich beavers, otters, martins [sic], and foxes are found there." In 1624, 7,246 beaver and 850 otter pelts were shipped from New Netherlands for a total value of 28,000 guilders. By 1633 8,800 beaver and 1,383 otter pelts returned 90,000 guilders, while the accumulated trade for 1634 and 1635 brought 135,000 guilders.

The Iroquois enjoyed an enviable position of being the middle men between the Dutch traders and the hinterlands where the furs were collected, and they expanded their territory in their search for ever greater supplies. But as the numbers of pelts delivered to the Dutch increased, local resources decreased, and the Iroquois had to range further and further afield. By 1640 the Iroquois had utterly exhausted their own supplies of beaver. It seems likely that by the middle of the seventeenth century there was not a living beaver in what is now the state of New York except in the remote Adirondacks, and most certainly the population of beaver even there had been seriously depleted by Iroquois and Algonquin trappers.

Other Indians were experiencing similar shortages. The *Jesuit Relation* for 1634 reports that the Hurons had exhausted their supplies of native beaver and the Montaignais were about to do the same. The Indians who traded with both the French and the Dutch had to look further west for beaver. When Adriaen Van der Donck wrote in 1655 that there were "multitudes of beavers" in New Netherlands, he meant that there was a multitude of beaver pelts passing through New Netherlands, for he writes later in the same account that, "The beavers are mostly taken far inland, there being few of them near the settlements." Still, by the 1680s 80,000 beaver pelts a year were being shipped out of New Netherlands.

By the end of the seventeenth century, the focus of the fur trade was moving steadily westward as the eastern beaver population was destroyed. Occasional Indians no doubt trapped in the Adirondacks, but the fact that the terrain made it difficult to secure skins and then get them out suggests that the activity was probably minimal. To be sure, Thomas Pownall's map of 1776 hints that the Iroquois were trapping in the Adirondacks. Across the region was this inscription: "This vast Tract of Land, which is the Antient Couchsachrage, one of the Four Beaver Hunting Countries of the Six Nations, is not yet Surveyed." But since Pownall had elsewhere written of the reluctance or inability of the Indians to describe this country, it seems likely that trapping there was negligible.

* * *

Throughout the period of the fur trade, there appears to have been little awareness of the finitude of nature's resources. Even though Europeans had depleted their own native supplies of pelts by the fifteenth century, they did not apply the obvious lesson of this ecological calamity to America. The literature of the first New Yorkers abounds with the impression that the wildlife of New Netherlands was infinite in quantity and able to withstand virtually endless exploitation. There were exceptions — some early writers recognized that nature could run out — but they were, literally, voices of those crying in the wilderness.

WILDLIFE AND WILDERNESS

When Champlain first entered the lake that bears his name, he was amazed at the great quantities of wild game on the islands and shores. His party saw and captured "an abundance of fowl, and such animals of the chase as stags, fallow-deer, fawns, roe-bucks, bears, and others." The ubiquity of beaver also impressed him. Emanuel van Meteren in his account of Hudson's voyage up the Hudson to the Mohawk wrote that the Dutch found "friendly and polite people, who had an abundance of provisions, skins, and furs, of martens and foxes, and many other commodities."

Throughout many of the first accounts we find the general impression that the New World was a land of plenty filled with uncountable numbers of animals. In 1625 Johan de Laet wrote that the new land was especially suitable for settlement "since it seems to lack nothing that is needful for the subsistence of man." The pervasiveness of this impression testified, among other things, to the care with which the Indians had treated their resources. But it was not long before the numbers of certain species in certain areas began to diminish. Beaver were not the only animals showing signs of excessive exploitation.

In 1644 Johannes Megapolensis, a Dutch minister who lived among the Mohawks for several years, published an account of the Indians and their country. He described some alarming changes in the relative abundance of wildlife since the coming of the white man:

> The year before I came here [1641], there were so many turkeys and deer that they came to feed by the houses and hogpens, and were taken by the Indians in such numbers that a deer was sold to the Dutch for a loaf of bread, or a knife, or even for a tobacco pipe; but now one commonly has to give for a good deer six or seven guilders.

Despite the observation that the numbers of this species had decreased, Megapolensis went on to describe a number of other species that the Dutch were killing in enormous numbers—including passenger pigeons, which he said the Dutch could bring down at the rate of fifty a shot—without the slightest suspicion that what had happened with the deer could happen again.

Adriaen Van der Donck also catalogued the animals of New Netherlands, suggesting that they were practically numberless. Yet we know that by the time he wrote there must have been a noticeable decline in the populations of certain species. The progress of the Iroquois wars, moreover, demonstrates that the Iroquois, by then dependent on the Dutch trade for newly appreciated luxuries, spread themselves further from Fort Orange (Albany) in their search for pelts.

Deer, wrote Van der Donck, were "incredibly numerous... and the Indians kill many thousands.... Venison is so easily obtained that a good buck cashes for five guilders." He was apparently unaware that just a little over a decade before, the deer were so numerous that they were selling for a much lower price. Further in his report Van der Donck admitted,

> There are some persons who imagine that the animals of the country will be destroyed in time, but this is unnecessary anxiety. It has already continued many years, and the numbers brought in do not diminish. The country is full of lakes, rivers, seas, streams, and creeks, and extends very far, even to the great south sea; hence we infer that there will not be an end to the wild animals, and also because there are large districts where the animals will remain unmolested.

At least a few of the Dutch settlers were early conservationists — to the extent that they objected to excessive exploitation — but the politicians, like Van der Donck, ignored their warnings. If he had taken the trouble to examine the statistics of the quantities of furs passing through the colony, partially cited above, he would have discovered dramatic evidence that the "numbers brought in" *were* diminishing, although the profits — the matter of most significance — were not. And if he had taken the further trouble to learn exactly where the furs passing through New Netherlands had originated, he would have realized that nearly all came increasingly from the territory far to the west.

By 1671 Governor de Courcelles of New France could write, "It is well known that the Iroquois nations, especially the four upper ones, do not have any beaver or elk. They absolutely exhausted the side of Ontario which they inhabit, that is, the South side, a long time ago." Baron LaHontan also recorded the scarcity of game among the Iroquois, who possessed, wrote the baron, "a pleasant and fertile country; but they want Roe-Bucks and Turkeys." He made this observation in 1694 and repeated it later in a summary chapter outlining his reasons why the Iroquois could be persuaded to forsake their alliance with the English (who by this time had replaced the Dutch in New York) and become allies of the French. He argued that the Iroquois had no venison in their native land, could not supply their large trading parties sufficiently for the long trip to New York, and could therefore be easily induced to make the shorter journey to a French outpost on Lake Ontario.

How could this have happened? If contemporary scholars like Calvin Martin are right in arguing that native Americans lived in harmony with their environment in the years before the arrival of Europeans, what forces were at work to lead the Iroquois and other Indians to destroy the capacity of nature to support them? The answer to this perplexing riddle, according to Martin, is that the impact of white civilization on Indian culture was in every way pernicious. Whereas the lives of pre-contact Indians had been characterized by stability, association with whites introduced devastating diseases, such as smallpox and a host of others, to which Indians had no natural resistance. In addition to the horrors of plague-like epidemics that wiped out whole villages, there were more subtle assaults on the predictable social and cultural patterns they had known for centuries. These included alcohol and the strange new customs of a commercial economy.

As the combination of disease and the corrupting effects of an emerging capitalist economy altered Indian life forever, many Indians concluded that the wild animals, on which their existence had always depended, had betrayed the sacred connection between humans and the rest of nature. As a consequence, populations of beaver, deer, and other important species were virtually wiped out. This is not to say that Indian culture would otherwise have survived. The deleterious effects of disease, alcohol, and avarice had already destroyed whatever chance the New York Indians had of protecting their ancient culture against the newcomers. It should also be repeated that Martin's thesis is not universally accepted; other historians see the Iroquois willingness to wipe out beaver populations simply as a function of the introduction of a market economy. In this view the Indian claim that animals had broken faith was merely a rationalization for succumbing to seductive economic forces.

* * *

The depletion of game in that part of New York outside the Adirondacks continued into the eighteenth century. In 1705 the citizens of the province were constrained to accept a closed season on deer for the first time, and it became illegal to hunt deer from January 1 to August 1. Although this law was probably never strictly enforced, it carried a penalty of twenty shillings for violations.

Peter Kalm, a Swedish naturalist who traveled extensively in America in the mid-eighteenth century, wrote that Albany was still very much a center of the fur trade but that the furs came from the western part of the colony. In his travels Kalm crossed what is now the Blue Line into the Adirondacks. From what he says about the region it is clear that by then, at least, Indians were trapping there—enough, anyway, to justify Governor Pownall's later description of it as an Indian hunting ground. Kalm called the territory west of Lake Champlain a wilderness and declared, "Not a human being lives in these waste regions and no Indian villages are found there. It is a land still left to wild animals, birds, etc." But certain Indians, he observed, hunted there in the fall, especially for deer and beaver. If the Indians were hunting deer and beaver in the area west of Lake George, as Kalm said, then they were probably some of the only hunters in the eastern part of New York meeting with any success.

Kalm was particularly interested in direct observation of American wildlife. Among the mammals that Kalm sighted in the Adirondacks—and Kalm's descriptions are the first accounts of animals actually seen in what is now the Adirondack region—were wolves, bears, squirrels, deer, and muskrats. Because of the increasing traffic on the Lake George-Champlain route at this time there must have been concomitantly increasing hunting pressure on the wildlife in this corner of the Adirondacks. Because of its proximity to a trade route and to a relatively large population center in Albany, the area around Lake George was probably the first fringe of the Adirondacks to be penetrated by white men.

During the long period of war, starting with the French and Indian War and finally ending with the American Revolution, the fur trade and most commercial hunting were sharply curtailed, but as soon as hostilities ceased, the wildlife of New York, including the Adirondacks, began to experience pressure as never before. The next hundred years would see radical changes in the Adirondack wildlife community, and it did not take long for them to start. By 1796, for example, Jonathan Wright, a trapper, could no longer make a living around Lake George. Acknowledging the need to exercise some protection of natural resources, in 1788 the new state of New York reestablished the closed season on deer from January 1 to August 1. This law also prohibited the use of hounds in hunting deer and provided a fine of three pounds for violations.

3 The John Cheney Era

In 1798 JEDIDIAH MORSE, compiler of *The American Gazeteer*, wrote of New York State, "In the northern and unsettled parts of the state are plenty of moose, deer, bears, some beavers, martins [sic], and most other inhabitants of the forest." Morse thus emphasized the abundance typically associated with an area largely unknown and unexplored. In fact, the wildlife of the Adirondacks was abundant only when compared with that of the rest of the state and that only because settlers had killed so many of the native animals or destroyed their habitat. Before the white man arrived in what became New York, the wildlife of the Adirondacks was relatively sparse, but by the time Euro-Americans moved into the area in significant numbers, the Adirondacks held a substantial portion of the state's remaining animal populations.

After the American Revolution, when settlers were leaving the coastal towns and agricultural areas, looking for better lives on the frontier, a few of the heartier (or less well informed) chose the relatively inhospitable Adirondacks. Not many stayed for long. They soon found that the Adirondack growing season offered a farmer little more than a marginal existence, but those who did stay cleared a few acres. Keene Valley was settled by at least one family by 1797; by the first decade of the nineteenth century early settlers were cultivating subsistence farms around what would soon be known as the Fulton Chain; the Saranac Lakes area had its first settlers a few years later; Newcomb, in the heart of the Adirondacks, supported a farm by 1816; the Indian Sabacl may have settled at Indian Lake long before that; and Long Lake had farms on its shores by the 1830s. Despite these scattered settlements, the Adirondacks remained largely unexplored. In *The Last of the Mohicans*, published in 1826, James Fenimore Cooper wrote, with some exaggeration, that the "sterile and rugged district which separates the tributaries of Champlain from those of the Hudson, the Mohawk, and the St. Lawrence" is "even to this day, less known to the inhabitants of the [United] States, than the deserts of Arabia, or the steppes of tartary."

Coupled with these early, mostly futile, attempts at farming was the first penetration of the Adirondacks by lumberjacks. Before the Revolution white pine had been taken from the fringes of the region, but trees were cut only when they were conveniently close to a sawmill. In 1813, however, Norman and Alanson Fox tried the then novel idea of cutting timber far from the mill and floating it down stream, in this case down the Schroon River from Brant Lake to the Hudson and Glens Falls. Their example was quickly followed, and for many years the Hudson was a major conduit for logs leaving the Adirondacks and destined for the great mills at Glens Falls. Eventually, nearly every Adirondack river served as a logging artery, carrying logs from the forested interior in all directions to mill towns like Ticonderoga, Lyons Falls, Potsdam, and Ogdensburg.

Nineteenth-century loggers had an important impact on wildlife both with the timber they actually cut and removed and with the forest fires that sometimes succeeded their operations. It was not until early in the present century that most lumberjacks or lumber companies began to display serious concern about the disastrous fires that occasionally raged over recently cut acreage. When those early loggers worked over an area, they cut only the big pines. The worthless branches were lopped off and left in the woods, where they soon became inflammable tinder. A careless hunter or a spark from a locomotive could start a forest fire deep in the woods.

This pattern of logging and fires began slowly. Even at the end of the nineteenth century, vast parcels of the Adirondacks had been barely cut. Nonetheless, early farms and lumbering operations meant that for the first time since the last glacier parts of the Adirondacks were opened up to sunlight and second growth timber. Young trees were sprouting new buds close enough to the ground for deer to reach them. During the first half of the nineteenth century, the deer population began to increase in the Adirondacks, where it has been maintaining an often difficult existence ever since. As each part of the Adirondacks was penetrated by farmers and lumberjacks, a few hundred acres here and a few hundred there were cleared or burned over and thus offered, after a few years, good deer browse.

* * *

WILDLIFE AND WILDERNESS

When Timothy Dwight was traveling through eastern New York in 1802, he stopped at Lake George. His narrative of this excursion supplies perhaps the first description of deer hunting inside what is now the Blue Line. The method, a variation of the old Indian practice of driving deer to water, was new to Dwight:

> The huntsmen with their hounds rouse [the deer] from their retreats in the forest, when they immediately betake themselves to the water, and swim toward the opposite shore. Other huntsmen engaged in the business place themselves on the points to watch their entrance into the lake. Each of these is provided with a small, light bateau, which he is able to row faster than the deer can swim. When he has overtaken the deer, he dispatches him with a stroke, or two, of his oar, and then tows him back to the beach.

Driving deer to water with hounds was a common and often controversial and illegal practice in the Adirondacks for nearly a hundred years after this account. Some hunters thought it was cowardly and inhumane, while others believed it to be the only manly way to take a deer. In the latter part of the century passionate discussions of the question filled the pages of popular sporting journals, and "hounding" deer, which was technically illegal when Dwight observed this hunt, would be alternately legalized and then prohibited every few years, until finally declared illegal for the last time near the end of the century.

The techniques of hounding were generally as Dwight described them: hounds were put out on the scent of deer and expected to drive them to a lake where hunters waited on the shore or in boats. To escape the hounds, some deer took to the water. Once the deer began swimming, the hunters could easily catch it: a well-rowed boat can always move more swiftly than a deer can swim. Usually, the hunters shot the deer with rifles or shotguns, but beating it over the head with a paddle or oar while someone else held its tail was not unusual. Around Lake George, wrote Dwight, bears were hunted in the same fashion, though they were always shot rather than beaten with oars, "being too dangerous to be closely approached."

Dwight participated in a deer drive and found himself to be no match for the Lake George native in enthusiasm for the hunt and joy in its success. At the sound of the hounds racing toward the lake, wrote Dwight, his guide

> instantly took fire. His eye kindled; his voice assumed a loftier tone; his stride became haughty; his style swelled into pomp; and his sentiments were changed rapidly from mildness to ardor, to vehemence and to rage.... I was forcibly struck with the sameness of the emotions produced by hunting and by war.

The sentimental Dwight was disturbed by the sight of the dead buck when it was heaved into the boat and stowed on the bottom beside him, writing that the deer possessed "an eye of as affecting supplication as I almost ever beheld." Indeed, he added, to him it evinced more the "attitude of a suffering infant than can easily be conceived." This picture stuck with him for years, and he remained shocked by the attitude of the local hunters, who, we should remember, were hunting not for sport but for food for themselves and their families.

Currier and Ives, "Lake George, Black Mountain" (undated).
(Collection Adirondack Museum)

* * *

Two outstanding Adirondack hunters and trappers of those years of early settlement were described by Jeptha R. Simms in his *Trappers of New York*: these were Nick Stoner and Nat Foster. Major Nicholas Stoner, an army veteran from the Revolution, was one of the first white men to trap and hunt in northern Fulton and southern Hamilton counties, and for years he ran trap lines along the lower Sacandaga River. He carried traps for beaver, otter, and muskrat, as well as a four-foot-long monster designed for bears, which drove spikes through the leg of a bear caught in it. In one spring he trapped twenty-six beavers and five otters — a good catch, prime beaver pelts going for about four dollars and otter for from five to seven dollars. Stoner's biographer writes admiringly that in one season Stoner made over a hundred dollars from trapping.

Nat Foster, younger than Stoner, moved to Herkimer County from Vermont about ten years after the Revolution. Primarily a trapper, he supported himself and his wife selling large quantities of beaver, otter, muskrat, marten, and other furs. One season he was known to have had a trapline of four hundred muskrat traps. For years he was the most celebrated hunter in the region; Simms wrote that during his life Foster killed more game than other man in New York. In one year he killed seventy-six deer and over three seasons ninety-six bears.

Although by inclination a trapper, in some years Foster turned his attentions solely toward hunting deer, selling their skins and saddles (the portion of the venison containing the backbone and the two loins). When he could kill a moose, it was a valuable opportunity. As late as 1871 the Albany Museum displayed a moose hide that Foster had sold for fifty dollars. Jonathan Wright, a friend of both Stoner's and Foster's, once employed an unusual method for killing a moose. Out in the woods in early spring with a dog but not a gun, Wright was snowshoeing on a thick crust on deep snow. His dog cornered a moose in a yard, and the moose decided to make a fight of it instead of floundering in the drifts. Wright tied his hunting knife to the end of a long stick, sneaked up on the moose through a thicket, and hamstrung it. Unable to move, the moose was easily destroyed. On the same day Wright killed another moose by plunging the knife into its heart.

Two other contemporary hunters reported by Simms to have downed their share of game in their lifetimes were Elisha Risdon, who killed 579 deer over a period of twenty-eight years, and Thomas Meacham of St. Lawrence County who died in 1850, having killed 77 mountain lions, 214 wolves, 219 bears, and 2,550 deer. And this was long before the Adirondack deer herd reached its peak population.

* * *

The most famous of all the hunters of this era was John Cheney (1800-1877). He moved to the Newcomb area from Ticonderoga in about 1830, after finding the Lake Champlain region too civilized and game too scarce, and was hired by the proprietors of the McIntyre iron mine as guide, hunter, and factotum. Cheney's adventures are described in books by Charles Fenno Hoffman, Charles Lanman, and Joel T. Headley, all of whom greatly admired his prowess and mild demeanor. All three undoubtedly

THE JOHN CHENEY ERA

embellished the tales of his forest exploits. In 1837 Hoffman compared Cheney to James Fenimore Cooper's Natty Bumppo and declared that if Natty had not first appeared in 1824 he would have been sure that Cheney had been Cooper's model. Many an urban reader must have thrilled to dramatic tales about Cheney shooting fierce wolves and mountain lions.

Winslow Homer, "Trapping in the Adirondacks" (1870).
(Collection Adirondack Museum)

Cheney conducted most of his hunting to supply venison to the McIntyre employees and their families. He used a distinctive weapon that he had made after he had broken the stock of his rifle, which had misfired, over the head of an enraged wolf. Believing that a long rifle was unwieldy in the thick woods, he acquired a pistol with an eleven-inch barrel and a birch-root stock. With this peculiar gun and an assortment of traps he killed his game in the deep woods of Essex County. In his first thirteen years in the wilderness he was reported to have killed 600 deer, 400 martens, 19 moose, 48 bears, 30 otters, and several wolves, mountain lions, and beavers.

Cheney was outspoken when it came to his views on the proper way to hunt deer. A market hunter, one who hunted for a living rather than for recreation, he was nonetheless sensitive to matters of sportsmanship. "The only manly way to kill deer," he maintained to Lanman, "is by 'driving' them, as I do, with a couple of hounds." The other common methods of hunting deer he disdained as cowardly and unsporting:

> In the first place there's the "still hunting" fashion, where you lay in ambush near a salt lick and shoot the poor creatures, when they're not thinking of you. And there's the beastly manner of blinding them with a "torch light" when they come into the lakes to cool themselves, and get away from the flies, during the warm nights of summer. Now I say, that no decent man will take this advantage of wild game, unless he is in a starving condition.

However sportsmanly driving was in Cheney's mind, it was unquestionably efficient. Headley reported that Cheney killed seventy deer a year (Cheney's numbers, reported by a variety of writers, do not always add up). He was helped considerably by a few well-trained dogs. He had one dog, Buck, who by the time he was four years old had helped his master bag several hundred deer. A few decades later, Charles Dudley Warner, unimpressed by the arguments for the sportsmanship of hounding, observed, "The dogs do the hunting, the men the killing."

A controversial variation of driving was withing, wherein the hunter, before going out onto the water, cut down a birch sapling and stripped off all except the two uppermost branches. These he twisted together so as to have a loop at the end of the pole. After the hounds had driven a deer to water, the hunter pursued it by boat as usual, but instead of grabbing it by the tail or shooting it, he dropped the noose over the deer's head and drowned it by holding it under water. Linus Catlin, a companion of Cheney's, withed a deer when Hoffman was visiting the iron works, and Cheney made no secret of his contempt for the practice, commenting "I never see any good in withes."

The debate between the advocates of driving deer and simple stalking, or still-hunting, was a fierce one and was not settled until long after Cheney's death. Both sides believed they stood for sportsmanship and humanity to animals, but it seems probable that hunters chose sides only after they had decided which method worked best for them. The still-hunters accused the hounders of not being able to take a deer without the help of snarling hounds who frightened every deer in the area before one finally took to water. The drivers, on the other hand, argued that the still-hunters were a sneaky crew who baited unsuspecting deer with salt licks and shot them before they knew the hunt was on.

A third practice, often classed with still-hunting, but equally disdained by hounders, including Cheney, was jacking. Hunters set out in boats on a lake or river after dark and paddled close to the shore. In the bow stood a jacklight, a stick holding a candle or small torch. A piece of birch bark or some other shield kept the light from shining on the hunters. Deer drinking or feeding on aquatic plants would be mesmerized by the light and unable to see the men, who could paddle up to within a few feet of the deer — so long as they were absolutely quiet.

Since the best season for jacking is during the summer, many of the deer killed along the lake shores were undoubtedly does still nursing fawns. Another reason why it was considered particularly cruel was that a deer might be wounded, make its way into the woods, and collapse. But the hunters, in the dark, would never know it. Jacking enjoyed a much greater popularity later in the century when it became fashionable for city sports to spend a few weeks in the North Woods. Often poor shots and poorer woodsmen, many of these men could never have killed a deer without guides who paddled them up to within easy shooting range. Nonetheless, Thomas Bangs Thorpe claimed that in jacking, "many of the best requisites of the sportsman are called out." Although jacking came to be associated largely with vacationing urban sport hunters, it began early in the nineteenth century among the first settlers.

The feuds between the different types of hunters were finally resolved by the legislature, but not before many of the hunters of the Eastern United States had been divided into hostile camps. Even in Cheney's day there were families living at the McIntyre iron works who refused to associate with people who hunted differently from themselves. Hoffman wrote that their "interminable bickerings" were worthy of an epic poet and reminded him of classic political contests of the middle ages. During the Cheney era the arguments centered on sportsmanship and manliness. A few decades later, each side would accuse the other of killing too many deer and at the wrong time of the year, thus endangering the very existence of the Adirondack deer herd.

* * *

One of the first political actions taken by early settlers was the establishment of bounties on wolves and mountain lions. The state of New York did not pay bounties on these animals before 1871, but the towns nearly always did. Wells in Hamilton County, for example, paid at least four bounties on wolves as early as 1811. The minutes of a Long Lake town meeting for 1837 illustrate the common attitude: "it was voted to rais mouney on the town to pey ten dollars on every wolf and panther full groon and five dollars on whelps."

Mountain lions and wolves were considered vermin, unnatural beasts not fit to live near human settlements. In the minds of the early Adirondack settlers they symbolized everything uncivilized, feral, and cruel. Every missing sheep or hog was blamed on them. It is questionable whether the value of livestock killed by wolves and mountain lions in the Adirondacks equalled the amount of bounty money paid for the heads of these predators, but the settlers, certain that their stock was being depleted by the predation of wolves and mountain lions, saw bounties as the solution. Professional trappers saw an opportunity for a quick buck. Nat Foster was reputed to have killed twelve wolves in one night near Limekiln Falls, and Nick Stoner made it a practice always to have traps out for wolves. Some time around 1825 Foster killed twenty-five wolves in a year and received 1250 dollars in bounties. He was probably collecting money from both the town and the county in which the wolves were killed.

* * *

In 1836, as part of the New York Natural History Survey, James E. DeKay was named state zoologist. In 1840 he and other scientists took a long canoe trip through the Adirondack wilderness, passing from Lake Pleasant to Raquette Lake via a winding network of rivers, lakes, and ponds and some difficult carries. The wildlife that he spotted on this trip and on other excursions or heard about from the local trappers and guides he catalogued in his monumental *Zoology of New York; Or, the New York Fauna*. This two-volume work, which appeared over a three-year period (1842-44), constituted the first effort to describe all the animal species in New York and the earliest serious examination of Adirondack wildlife. It also became the model for similar projects undertaken in other states.

Especially important are DeKay's remarks on the Adirondack species that were rare or extirpated in the rest of the state and were soon to become endangered in the Adirondacks. The wolverine, he wrote, was "still found in the districts north of Raquet [sic] Lake." He further asserted that the wolverine is a "very troublesome and destructive animal." (Wildlife biologist C. H. D. Clarke says that this is the type of "old nonsense" that caused the wolverine to become extirpated in the Adirondacks in the first place.) Wolverines must have been quite scarce by this time; only two years earlier DeKay had assumed in a preliminary report that they had been eliminated from New York.

The lynx was "not uncommon in the northern districts." This animal, DeKay admitted, killed some livestock but mostly lived on rabbits and other small mammals. Bobcats (which he called wild cats) were extirpated from most of the state except the western counties and the Adirondacks. In colonial times there had been a bounty on bobcats, and they are still considered vermin by many hunters. The other Adirondack cat, the mountain lion, persisted in Hamilton, Herkimer, and St. Lawrence counties. DeKay rejected the many stories of mountain lions' attacking humans and asserted that he had never "met with a well authenticated account of their having attacked a man." By the 1840s wolves had disappeared from all of New York except the northwestern Adirondacks and St. Lawrence County. Lending too much credence to the stories of Adirondack hunters, DeKay claimed that wolves threatened the deer population, killing five for every one shot by a man.

The fur bearers all survived, but some species were becoming scarce. The Adirondack otter remained plentiful enough to be trapped and by DeKay's time was worth eight dollars for a good pelt. Fisher were common only in Hamilton County but were found scattered in the rest of the northern part of the state. Marten could be found throughout the state, as could mink.

Beaver were rare and near extirpation. On the canoe trip of 1840, DeKay saw several signs but no live beaver. He believed that soon they would be gone from the entire eastern United States and that the last ones would persist in remote pockets of the Adirondacks. In 1815, reported DeKay, a party of St. Regis Indians from Canada traveled up the Oswegatchie River after that area had been relatively undisturbed for several years because of the war between the United States and Great Britain. After a few weeks they returned with three hundred beaver pelts. Subsequently, he was told, "very few have been observed." In 1840 there were scattered beaver families in the northern part of Hamilton, the southern part of St. Lawrence, and the western part of Essex counties. In 1844 John Cheney told Headley that he knew of but one beaver colony.

Probably a discovery made in South America around 1820 saved the Adirondack beaver from complete extirpation. At that time, furriers discovered that the fur of the coypu, a large aquatic rodent similar to the beaver but without the flat tail, offered a pelt nearly the equal of a beaver's.

James DeKay, "The Moose," *Zoology of New York: Or, the New York Fauna* (1844).

This fur, known as nutria, quickly became a major item in the international fur business and may have saved the life of many a North American beaver. Beaver peltry remained merchantable on the open market and was still sought, but the discovery of the coypu may have saved the North American beaver from extinction.

James DeKay, "The Beaver," *Zoology of New York: Or, the New York Fauna* (1844).

DeKay reported that deer were still common throughout the state, although they were becoming scarce around population centers and had been extirpated on Long Island. He observed that they were rare in the most northern parts of the Adirondacks and blamed wolf predation. More likely, the early logging and farming responsible for clearing parts of the Adirondacks were still concentrated around the Hudson River watershed.

During the 1820s (according to historian Charles Snyder, writing at the end of the century) moose had been so common around Old Forge that the settlers' children kept a tame one as a pet. Two decades later, wrote DeKay, they were "yet numerous in the unsettled portions of the state, in the counties of Essex, Herkimer, Hamilton, Franklin, Lewis, and Warren." DeKay believed that since the moose was no longer being hunted by Indians it was actually on the increase, but this seems unlikely. The Adirondack moose was beginning its steady decline toward extirpation. Less than twenty years after DeKay completed his report, the last native Adirondack moose was killed. The moose's chances were not improved when a hunter in southern Hamilton County at about DeKay's time sold two live moose to a menagerie "for a round sum." Sporting writer C. W. Webber noted that this windfall "set all the hunters in a furor to capture live moose."

Before the sportsmen from the cities began to come to the Adirondacks, most of the local hunters bagged moose during the winter when they yarded up in a relatively protected area and with normal movement kept the snow trampled down. Hoffman described what happened when one such yard was discovered on the property of the McIntyre iron works. Several hunters came upon a cow and two yearlings in a yard and proceeded to shoot wildly, wounding but not bringing them down. The moose tried to charge the hunters, who stood safely on their snowshoes on the surrounding drifts. As the moose floundered in the deep snow, the hunters bludgeoned them with axes or clubs. "The two yearlings, with their dam, after making a most gallant resistance, were ultimately dispatched."

Harvey Holt, one of John Cheney's fellow hunters at the iron works, showed a particular inclination for killing moose. A letter from David Henderson to Archibald McIntyre (March 27, 1837) suggests the concern of the mine's owners over Holt's passion for hunting moose. Learning that Holt had just killed five moose, a dismayed Henderson, who hoped to promote the moose population, wrote that he wished that Holt had killed only one or two. Two years later, Archibald McIntyre wrote to mine employee Andrew Porteous that "Harvey Holt is a very steady man through the year, yet in the winter, if a favorable season occur, he always takes a Moose Hunt. Overlook that, however."

Into the 1840s moose remained relatively common. Writing from the vicinity of the iron works, Headley reported that during the previous spring two Indians had killed eighteen moose, and one of the hunters to whom Headley spoke said that he had killed three in a single day in March. Headley also wrote that he knew of old bulls eight feet tall. John Cheney, warning Lanman of the dangers involved in hunting moose, asserted that they were still quite numerous around Long Lake and Lake Pleasant in 1847. Cheney boasted to Lanman that one day near Mount Marcy he had killed two large bulls before nine o'clock in the morning. He discovered the moose in a winter yard, climbed up on a fallen log about ten feet off the ground, and shot both from the safety of his perch.

DeKay insisted that elk were still to be found in New York and repeated a story told to him by the hermit Beach, who lived for a while on Raquette Lake: Beach claimed that he had killed an elk in 1836 on the Saranac River. C. Hart Merriam conducted a survey similar to DeKay's in the 1880s and explicitly rejected Beach's claim to have killed an elk on the Saranac River or anywhere near it, observing, "I have never been able to find a hunter in this wilderness, however aged, who had ever heard of a living Elk in the Adirondacks."

J. MacDonald, "Hunting on Snow-Shoes" (1884).
(Collection Adirondack Museum)

* * *

As the first sportsmen prepared to make the journey north to the Adirondack wilderness, the wildlife community was changing, but sportsmen, preoccupied with deer, seldom noticed. Beaver were few and hard to find. The large predators, the wolf and mountain lion, were declining in numbers and range, and the moose would be gone by the time of the Civil War. But the major change — at least as far as the sportsmen were concerned — was the slowly increasing quantity of deer. And as long as the deer appeared to be plentiful, other animals seemed equally so. The romantic inclination to believe in abundance was typified in a comment of Headley's: "Game of all kinds swarm the forest; bears, wolves, panthers, deer, and moose."

It was an irony of history that the environmental changes resulting from logging and settlement happened to promote a species, the white-tailed deer, just then becoming popular as the object for a gentleman's sport. By the end of the nineteenth century, when the people of New York chose to save what was then left of the Adirondack wilderness, the deer was well established in fact and in story as the predominant game species. From the 1840s, through the establishment of the Forest Preserve, and right up to the present, the white-tailed deer has been, in the popular mind, the representative Adirondack animal.

A. F. Tait, "A Good Time Coming" (1862).
(Collection Adirondack Museum)

4 Sportsmen and the Hunt

BEGINNING IN THE 1830s, the Adirondacks became one of the most popular hunting and fishing grounds in the East. Gentleman sportsmen from Boston, New York, Philadelphia, and other Eastern cities repaired to the wilderness for several weeks of shooting white-tailed deer and catching trout. From this tradition developed a huge body of travel and sporting narratives. Articles and books by Joel T. Headley, A. B. Street, S. H. Hammond, Thomas Bangs Thorpe, and many others were typical of the genre. They invoked all the motifs of popular romanticism, while implying that the glories of the wilderness were accessible only to the soul properly sensitive to the aristocratic conventions of field sports.

"A Good Time Coming," an 1862 painting of an Adirondack wilderness campsite by Arthur Fitzwilliam Tait, where the sportsman, wearing a necktie, pours himself a cup of champagne, emphasizes the genteel characteristics of field sports in the Adirondacks. Recreational hunting and fishing were part of an aristocratic tradition, and urban hunters and anglers behaved as if the wilderness and its inhabitants existed solely for their private pleasure. The arrival of the sport hunter (even as subsistence and professional hunting continued), moreover, proved to be enormously important to the future of the Adirondacks. It suggested that the relationship of the Adirondack region, including its wildlife, to the rest of New York and to the Eastern United States would be largely based on recreation.

The literature of sport hunting is prodigious. Without delving into it in detail, I want to emphasize the distinction between subsistence hunting—what Timothy Dwight observed at Lake George and what Cheney and others were doing in the years before the arrival of sportsmen—and sport hunting. Hunting for sport has its own rituals and values, and it demonstrates an attitude toward nature, ideas about the human relationship to the rest of nature, quite different from that involved in subsistence hunting. It would be easy to suggest that hunting for survival, the kind of hunting conducted by the Indians, was somehow purer, nobler than hunting for sport, but I hope to avoid such an oversimplification. Sport hunting as such is no more to be condemned (in my view, at least) than backpacking is. Both hunters and hikers are trying to establish an intimacy with the natural world often elusive in a modern, urban society. The sport hunter who pursues his or her game with respect and with awareness of the dignity of the life taken has nothing to be ashamed of. The white-tailed deer shot by a hunter has certainly enjoyed a better life than the average beef-producing steer has. And it provides healthier meat.

But the differences between sport and subsistence hunting should not be minimized. To examine these differences, I begin with what may seem an obscure illustration. In the British Museum are huge slabs of sculpture taken from the ruins of Assyrian palaces in the country now known as Iraq. One series of these mammoth sculptures depicts the hunting exploits of an Assyrian king, Ashurbanipal, who built a new palace for himself at Nineveh in about 645 B.C. Considered by many scholars as the supreme achievement of Assyrian art, these sculptures record, in a series of dramatic narrative scenes, a ceremonial lion hunt. The important point of these sculptures for our purposes is that they clearly show a hunt conducted not for food or to control dangerous predators but for personal, symbolic purposes, in this case to accent royal authority and power.

The lions are released from cages in order for the king to chase and then kill them. No tracking or other outdoor skills, except for marksmanship with a bow, is required. More than anything else, the sculptures celebrate the vigor and royalty of the king himself; they emphasize his pride in an individual achievement. The only other royal exploit given treatment as extensive in similar sculptures is conquering foreign nations. Throughout, the hunting sculptures emphasize the king's prowess, his personal triumphs, his regal stature among his people. I believe that these sculptures tell us something important about the attitudes toward nature that eventually prevailed in the West, mainly that successful hunting was a personal accomplishment, a source of pride, and a triumph.

The absence of woodcraft in these illustrations, of course, is not necessarily typical of recreational hunting; one of the skills in which many modern hunters take the most pride is their woodcraft. More than the kill, their ability to track, read the woods, and understand their prey's natural behavior is the major source of their sense of accomplishment. Nonetheless, despite the artificiality of a hunt where the prey are released from cages, the Assyrian hunt reminds us of the difference between hunting for sport and hunting for food.

If Calvin Martin and others are correct in asserting the spiritual affinity expressed by the Northeastern American Indian with the animals he killed, then the critical difference between the Native American ideal of hunting and the values delineated by the Assyrian sculptures is that between a human who senses the innate equality and dignity of the animal killed and one who demonstrates and emphasizes his personal attributes in the hunt. Indian oral traditions, of course, suggest that Indians took pride in their woodcraft, and a common insult was to denigrate an enemy's hunting skills. But I believe that the source of their pride stemmed not so much from the successful kill as from their sense of kinship and empathy with the prey. The Assyrian sculptures celebrated the fierceness of the lions but only in order to magnify the message of the king's power. Ashurbanipal, we can infer, admired the strength, speed, and ferocity of the lions he killed, and he conducted his hunt with a great sense of ceremony, but he felt himself in one world and the lions in another.

* * *

The journalist Charles Fenno Hoffman appeared at the McIntyre iron works in September of 1839, about a month after reading that geologist Ebenezer Emmons, James DeKay's colleague on the Natural History Survey, had led the first known ascent of (and had named) Mt. Marcy. Although he had hunted as a boy along the Sacandaga River in the southern Adirondacks, his visit to the mine signals the arrival of the sportsman in the central Adirondacks. Speaking of the inevitable changes that he foresaw and probably having John Cheney in mind, he noted that "the old race of hunters already begin to find a new employment as guides to the owners of lands." (Hoffman himself owned no land in the Adirondacks and certainly expected to pay for the services of a guide.) He remarked further that some of the original hunters were so disturbed by the prospect of an invasion of any level of civilization that they had headed for the still unviolated wilderness of the West. One veteran hunter of seventy complained bitterly that there was then a settlement within thirty miles of him but he was too old to move. But most of the hunters stayed and served as guides to the men from Eastern cities who came to the Adirondacks to hunt, fish, and camp.

The sports nearly always camped on or near the water. Arriving at the end of a road they would engage a guide to paddle them in a canoe or row them in a guideboat. Only a few were interested (as Hoffman was) in climbing Marcy or marveling at the sublimity of Indian Pass. They came to fish and shoot deer, and the deer were found near the water. Usually a party of sportsmen hired one guide for each member of the group, thus having in each boat one guide and one hunter. A typical trip might start at the Saranacs from which a party could make its way to the Raquette River, via

Theodore R. Davis, "Floating for Deer in the Adirondacks" (1868).
Collection Adirondack Museum

Indian Carry and Stony Creek, and the lakes accessible from it—Long, Raquette, Forked, Blue Mountain, Tupper, and, for the more adventurous, the lakes at the head of the Bog River. The guides did all the work. They lugged the boats over the carries, cooked all the meals, and on more than a few trips secured all the food. Depending on the skill and inclination of the sports, the usual methods for shooting deer were jacking or hounding. If hounding was preferred, the guide brought along his own dogs, which were paddled around in the boats, along with vast quantities of camping gear.

If the party wished to have deer driven to water, a guide would take a boatload of hounds to some point on the lake where he thought they might pick up a scent. There they were set loose while the guides sited their clients at various strategic points around the lake, waiting in the boats for a deer to appear. Sometimes it took hours for the dogs finally to find a deer that would head for water, and the hunters often complained of the boredom of sitting in a boat, pestered by mosquitoes and black flies, and hearing the hounds baying all over some nearby mountain without ever driving a deer

"Life in the Woods" (1867).
Collection Adirondack Museum

into the lake. Eventually, at least in most cases described in print, a deer did show itself and begin swimming across the lake. Then came what was typically described as an exciting chase as the sport lounged in the boat while his guide desperately tried to cut the deer off from the shore toward which it was swimming. Urging the guide to paddle faster and faster, the sport would begin to lower his sights on the deer. Often his first shot missed completely. While he reloaded, the guide would try to catch up to the deer. It was not unusual for the guide to grab the deer's tail and hold on while the sport kept missing—if he had the courage, that is, for occasionally a guide was shot in the hand by some tenderfoot attempting to put a ball through a deer's head. After a deer was killed, it was dragged back to camp where the guides dressed and cooked it while the sports passed around the brandy flask.

For those whose taste was jacking the waterways were perfectly suited. Often the hunters who were first to jump into the boats at dark were the same ones who had been out on the lake all day pursuing deer driven to water by hounds. As soon as the last glow of day had left the sky, the jackers were out in their boats. Here a guide's skill as a paddler was tested, for he had to paddle along the shore line without making a sound. Squinting at the shore for some sign of a deer drinking or feeding, the sport waited to light the jack. In some cases, the jack was a lantern in a contraption worn like a miner's helmet. A guide and his client might paddle for miles, up and down a river bank or lake shore without seeing a single deer, while the sport complained of tedium and bothersome insects.

But if a deer was sighted, it was all worth it. Joel T. Headley dramatically described the typical scene: "The deer, attracted by the flame, stops and gazes intently upon it. If he hears no sound he will not stir till you are close to him. At first you catch only the sight of his two eyes, burning like fire-balls in the gloom, but as you approach nearer, the light is thrown on his red flanks, and he stands revealed in all his beautiful proportions before you." The guide, if he was good, would paddle closer and closer, for the deer was dumfounded by the bright, moving light, utterly unable to see the hunter. As long as the deer did not hear anything, it usually would not make a move, but the slightest ripple of the paddle or the cocking of a gun and it was gone. Some guides would paddle their sports close to deer after deer only to see them miss their shots and the deer bound into the woods. In jacking there is no second shot.

* * *

The general impression with which one emerges from the sporting narratives of these years is of hunters who, with some exceptions, lacked woodcraft but were eager to kill. In *Arctic Dreams*, as part of an account of Eskimo hunting practices, Barry Lopez suggests that in the Eskimos' ethics the need for "dignified" relations between humans and animals developed. Throughout the literature of sport in the Adirondacks in the nineteenth century, it is not the killing or even the waste that startles. It is the lack of dignity, denied to both the hunters and the hunted.

It would be wrong to assume that the wasteful, exploitative attitudes toward nature displayed by many sportsmen were peculiar to them. The mid-nineteenth century was an age of expansion, and one of the dominant metaphors of the culture trumpeted the American mission to transform the wilderness into a garden. Wherever they looked, most Americans saw wild nature as the obstacle to the divinely ordained mandate of American civilization to tame the wilderness and settle the continent. They also believed that the natural resources of the new world were inexhaustible. Thus Adirondack sport hunters, for all their waste, merely represented the prevailing values of their culture; their assumptions about nature were shared by nearly all Americans. The waste in the Adirondacks, moreover, seems minimal when compared with that in regions where game was more abundant. In Francis Parkman's *The Oregon Trail*, for example, a narrative describing the adventures of a Boston aristocrat in the trans-Mississippi West in 1846, we find the author enthusiastically shooting buffalo after buffalo, his entire party slaughtering dozens simply for sport, occasionally taking some meat, but often leaving whole carcasses untouched.

The important point to be remembered is that whatever waste and arrogance were displayed by hunters in the Adirondacks stemmed not from the fact that these people were hunters but from their participation in the materialistic, expansive culture of nineteenth-century America. Those people who did come to hunt, moreover, went home having experienced nature in a way that others seldom did. As the historian John Reiger has argued in *American Sportsmen and the Origins of Conservation*, the first American conservationists often either were or had been hunters. They had seen the wilderness and its wild inhabitants, and some of them understood what America stood to lose if it continued to abuse its natural inheritance.

* * *

Although Adirondack sportsmen had fewer animals to hunt than Parkman did out on the prairie, examples of unnecessary killing routinely appear in the sporting literature. Consider the case of one correspondent to *Forest and Stream* who described a hunting expedition near Follensby Clear Pond some time in the 1850s, using the pen name "Zoophilus." Chasing a buck across the pond, exhorting his guide to row faster, he "admired the splendid antlers as they stood out from the head"; then he shot the deer from a respectable fifteen yards. The next day, before this deer was even cleaned, he spotted another buck in the lake. He paddled himself to the deer, shot it once, then clobbered it with an oar, and shot it again, this time through the neck. Somehow the buck made it to the shore where Zoophilus finally killed it with one more shot. Then his companions gathered around him for the ritual sharing of the flasks. All this carnage was recounted after Zoophilus had opened his article with a vituperative attack on the neophyte hunters crowding the woods at the time the piece was published in the 1870s.

Not all the hunters of this period were wasteful; a few condemned needless killing. Joel T. Headley met two men returning to Stony Creek Ponds from Ampersand Lake. The men admitted that they had killed five deer in five days, and Headley expressed indignation that they should have been so wasteful. One deer would have fed them well for five days, and they must have left the others to rot where they were shot. He observed, "This

Frederick Remington,
"A Good Day's Hunting in the Adirondacks" (1892).
Collection Adirondack Museum

is constantly done by men who visit this region in summer, and who call themselves sportsmen." He was told of one man, a clergyman (Headley himself was an ordained minister, but by the time he was camping in the Adirondacks he had turned to writing for a career), who had slaughtered so many deer in one unidentified section over a period of years that he was informed by the local settlers and guides that if he ever returned to the area it would be at the risk of his life.

Headley went on to editorialize at some length about measures that serious sportsmen should take to deal with such "common marauders." In addition to the "mere waste and brutality" of wanton killing, he noted, was the selfishness. According to him, when deer flesh is left to rot in the open it drives away the deer yet living. Hunters following their wasteful brethren and depending on the land to furnish them with their daily food would find the area worthless for hunting and any pleasure. True hunters, suggested Headley, should band together and see that abuses were prosecuted, but he admitted the difficulty in enforcement since any legal action would mean securing a writ from authorities that were often a hundred miles away through roadless wilderness.

Still the slaughter went on. Charles Fenton, who for many years was one of the best known hunters and hotel owners in the Adirondacks, described, in a brief article in *Forest and Stream*, a bloody afternoon on Vanderwhacker Mountain between Newcomb and Minerva. Still-hunting, alone, sometime in 1857, Fenton, first shot and killed a buck. Then he killed a doe nearby. Leaving both carcasses, he went on to look for more. He came upon a bear cub playing with its mother, and he shot the cub. His first shot at the mother only wounded her. He chased her, wounded her again, chased her some more, wounded her four more times, and finally brought her down, but not dead, with two more shots. The death blow came with a knife in the bear's breast. Not a morsel of all this meat was taken back to his camp, where he found his friends and "recited to them the exciting adventures of my day's hunt on Mount Vanderwhacker."

During this time, the forties and fifties, hotels began to appear throughout the Adirondacks at places convenient for hunting parties. Two of the most famous were Martin's and Bartlett's on the Saranac Lakes. When the local guides were not employed by sportsmen, they were hired by the hotels to supply them with venison. Since shooting deer before August was at least technically illegal, it was commonly indicated on the menu by the transparent euphemism "spring mountain lamb." It was a rare, and possibly poor, hotel that did not have venison available under one guise or another at any time of the year in the nineteenth century. A. B. Street, Adirondack writer and sportsman and New York State librarian, reported that Harvey Moody, one of the most famous of the Saranac guides, killed over a hundred deer in three weeks at Tupper Lake. Since this occurred before hostelries had been developed on Tupper Lake, Moody was probably working for one of the Saranac hotels.

* * *

Meanwhile, the debate over jacking continued. Most of its proponents were downstate sportsmen who needed all the help they could get to kill a deer. A few of the city sports, however, were persuaded by the guides that hounding was a fairer practice. Charles Lanman, who was probably won over to hounding by John Cheney, composed a condescending sketch of Steuben Hewitt, then the tenant of the Newcomb Farm. After floating for over an hour, Hewitt discovered a beautiful deer standing knee-deep in the water and looking back at him in stupefied wonder.

> The poor creature could see nothing before it but the mysterious light, and while standing in the most interesting attitude imaginable, the hunter raised his rifle and shot it through the heart. In a half an hour... I was lecturing the hard-hearted hunter on the cruelty of thus capturing the innocent creatures of the forest. To all my remarks, however, he replied, "They were given to us for food, and it matters not how we kill them."

Hounding, on the other hand, while not offering much sport to a man who was rowed by a guide to a swimming deer so he could put a bullet through its head while his guide held onto its tail, was not quite as simple as its opponents asserted. In the summer, argued hounding advocates, most deer are not afraid of dogs and will actually play with them a while, staying just out of their reach and gradually wearing them out. Dogs, like wolves, do not possess the stamina that deer have and usually will give up the chase when it looks like the deer is going to make a long run of it (in deep snow, of course, it is a different story).

Most important in a discussion of hounding deer is the question of whether hounded deer naturally take to water. Wildlife biologist C. H. D. Clarke, who hounded deer all his life in terrain in Ontario similar to that of the central Adirondacks, maintained that only wounded or sick deer will take to water to elude dogs. Contrary to the popularly held picture of dogs driving scores of fine bucks, their tongues hanging out in exhaustion, into a lake is Clarke's claim that he has seen dozens of deer calmly trotting through the woods, casually looking over their shoulders now and then to check on those annoying dogs.

Even when a dog was able to catch up to a deer, moreover, the deer still had a good chance. Lanman reported seeing a deer chased by five dogs to the edge of a cliff on Lake George. Turning, the deer decided to make a fight of it instead of leaping into the lake. Before the dogs' owners arrived and shot the deer, it had killed one dog and disabled another with its hoofs. Dogs on the loose in the winter can easily harass and even kill deer when the crust on the snow will support the dog with its broad pads but gives way under the sharp hoofs of a deer. Under those conditions packs of dogs can cause great damage to a deer herd, but in the summer and fall, when hounding traditionally occurred, a healthy deer did not have nearly as much to fear from a pack of hounds as it did from a guideboat with a torch set up in the bow.

* * *

Guideboat with sportsman, guide, hound, and dead deer, c. 1890.
Collection Adirondack Museum

During the 1830s and '40s the guideboat, an important material element in the history of Adirondack hunting, began its evolution toward the elegant craft it would become by the end of the nineteenth century. The long, closely joined water systems of the Adirondack wilderness made travel by boat more comfortable and convenient than by land. The Indians who had plied those waters before the white hunters and trappers replaced them had made and used the birchbark canoe. White hunters needed a craft that was light enough to be carried (in the Adirondacks, one never says *portage*) for two or three miles without wearing out the carrier; sturdy enough to hold two men, their gear, and maybe a dead deer; and sufficiently seaworthy to weather a storm in the middle of a large lake. The craft that eventually met all these demands was the Adirondack guideboat.

WILDLIFE AND THE WILDERNESS

Adirondack historian Alfred L. Donaldson credited Mitchell Sabattis and a member of the famous Palmer family for inventing the guideboat in Long Lake around 1840, but the foremost authorities on the subject, Kenneth and Helen Durant, whose *The Adirondack Guide-Boat* plumbs nearly every detail of this boat's history, design, and use, concluded that the boat evolved at various places throughout the lake country of the central Adirondacks and gradually became what we know today as the genuine guideboat.

From a distance the guideboat looks roughly like a canoe because like a canoe it has pointed ends. Unlike a canoe, however, a guideboat is rowed; this affords greater stability and better control. The construction of a guideboat was (and is) long and laborious, involving thin pine planks and thousands of tacks and screws. The stem and stern are made from the natural curve of a spruce knee, the part of the tree where the roots bend up into the stump. The many ribs are also fashioned from spruce knees, a tough, stiff wood found abundantly in the Adirondacks. The thin planks of the hull are primarily white pine and fastened with screws and tacks. Usually there are two pairs of oarlocks, one near the bow to be used when the rower has a passenger, who sat in the stern, and one near the center for when only one man is rowing. A further component of the guideboat's equipment is a yoke, which fits over the shoulders of whoever carries the boat and is similar to the yokes used by Adirondack and other farmers to carry pails of maple syrup.

The most prominent example of original, indigenous craftsmanship to come out of the Adirondacks, the guideboat emerged to meet the demands of geography and the times. It was the pickup truck of its day. While it was used by Adirondack natives for purposes as diverse as going to church or carrying produce to market, its builders were serving the needs of the guide, who required a craft in which he could conveniently transport gentleman hunters around the interlinking lakes of the Adirondacks. Hunting deer in this period was primarily conducted around bodies of water, and without the guideboat that hunting would have been perhaps too difficult for many city sports who came to the Adirondacks and wanted to bag a deer with as little effort as possible. Only if assisted by the guide's boat, dogs, and skill, was he able to secure his trophy.

* * *

How many deer were killed by men sitting in the stern of a guideboat cannot be known. At least one sportsman, however, was just as interested in seeing deer as he was in shooting them from behind a jacklight. This rarity among nineteenth-century Adirondack hunters was S. H. Hammond, author of two books on hunting and camping in the Adirondacks: *Hills, Lakes, and Forest Streams* (1854) and *Wild Northern Scenes* (1857). Hammond embarked on a long hunting trip in 1849 from Dannemora bound for the Chateaugay Lakes. On his first night, at Chazy Lake, he jacked a deer and thus provided himself and his guide with venison. The next night at

Currier and Ives, "The Life of a Sportsman" (1872).
Collection Adirondack Museum

Bradley Pond, about five miles deeper in the woods, he went out jacking again and saw a number of deer but did not fire a shot. "We had no occasion for venison, and we did them no harm that night." Later at Ragged Lake he went through the same ritual: late at night he set up the jack and went out on the lake solely for the purpose of looking at deer. The next day on the same lake he pursued a swimming deer clear across the lake, completely exhausting himself:

> we took no heed to the big drops of sweat that chased each other down our faces, as we pulled with might and main after him. Yet we had no thought of taking his life, — that we might easily have

done, for my loaded rifle lay in the bottom of our little craft. Our object was a trial of speed.

Hammond and the guide paddled right up to the frightened deer and actually touched it, but the rifle was never touched.

The combination of Hammond's more or less benign attitude toward deer, the anthropomorphism latent in the notion that the woods were teeming with "noble bucks," and the sentimentality inherent in Charles Lanman's condemnation of jacking illustrates the ambiguities of the mid-nineteenth-century American's response to all of nature. The deer were simultaneously a subject for intellectual scrutiny (as with Hammond), a resource to be exploited, and, as an ostensibly peaceful, herbivorous animal (as in Lanman's lament over the killing of "the innocent creatures of the forest"), a personification of nature's supposed bounty and goodness. At least one reason why Adirondack hunters and others argued so strenuously with one another about the proper way to hunt was that the deer was expected to fulfill so many diverse symbolic functions, and the reason for this, in turn, was that nineteenth-century Americans were confused about the relationship between themselves and nature.

* * *

Because so much of the literature about Adirondack wildlife in the mid-nineteenth century involved the white-tailed deer and sport hunting, documentation of the inevitable human interactions with the other animals is scarce. The people who wrote about the Adirondacks were, by and large, men from the cities whose primary interest was in hunting deer. Trappers were often illiterate and in any case were not inclined to write books about their exploits. The permanent settlers who tried to keep some kind of stock continued to worry about wolves, mountain lions, and bears but left only occasional records. From casual references and brief summaries in the books and articles by Street, Hammond, and their contemporaries, however, we can infer a general picture of the animals other than deer during the middle decades of the century.

DeKay noted in 1842 that beaver were becoming scarce. During the following years, this species continued to dwindle until some trappers thought it was extirpated in the Adirondacks. It appears now, however, that one or two colonies managed to survive in a couple of secluded areas until they were protected by law. In 1843, according to John Todd, the Long Lake area was still home for marten, mink, otter, and ermine, but beaver were rare and only a few were left. John Cheney devoted a fair share of his time to trapping and told Lanman that by 1847 he had trapped thirty otters and four hundred martens. Beaver, on the other hand, were so rare in that area that Cheney had trapped only one, and he thought that it was the last beaver to be taken in the state of New York.

The head of the Bog River, a wild and seldom penetrated spot, supported a beaver family sometime in the 1840s. Hammond noted that near the end of that decade the last of these was trapped. He believed that after that no beaver were left in the Adirondacks. By the late 1850s it is probable that the only beaver left in New York were confined to a small area around the St. Regis Lakes. Benson J. Lossing, author of a book about the Hudson River, learned in 1859 that two or three families of beaver had survived in the St. Regis region. Harvey Moody informed Street that he knew of a colony of beaver in the same place. When he and Street reached the St. Regis Lakes, they saw a beaver swimming across a lake. Moody shot at it but missed. Winslow Watson in his *History of Essex County* (1869) assumed that the beaver was extirpated in Essex County.

The smaller fur bearers were faring little better. In a description of the Adirondack wilderness for *Putnam's Monthly* in 1854, F. N. Benedict, an early surveyor and landowner, wrote that deer were numerous but marten, fisher, and beaver were rare. The fisher's popularity as a supplier of valuable furs rose and fell sporadically, but it was always killed when possible. Because the fisher often killed animals in traps and ruined pelts, most trappers considered it vermin. Harvey Moody told Street that he had devised a special trap just for fisher in order to keep them away from his dead falls for mink and marten, from which fisher were fond of stealing his bait. The trap was a snare which left the fisher hanging, alive, by one foot. Moody complained, moreover, of a general decrease in the quantity of fur bearers: "I ketched fisher and mink and sable [marten] and black foxes at Tupper's Lake, 'twixt sunrise and sundown, enough to kiver the little Bluebird [his boat] all over. But that can't be done now neither." In 1868 Street suggested that the wolverine still existed in the Adirondacks, but that seems unlikely.

* * *

The persecution of the large predators continued with redoubled strength as the small settlements in the interior Adirondacks grew in size and number. Nearly all the towns and counties in the Adirondacks established bounties on wolves and mountain lions. While the efficacy of the bounty system in actually controlling the numbers of predators is doubtful, it illustrates the fear and contempt the early settlers had for the wolf and mountain lion. By the middle of the century every town in Hamilton County, the least settled county in the Adirondacks, had bounties on both of these species. Persecution and the diminishing availability of truly wild habitat were pushing them deeper and deeper into the wilderness and would eventually eliminate them from the Adirondacks entirely.

Hammond's guide, Tucker, told him that mountain lions were just about all gone from the Adirondacks in 1849, but they did see one in a tree near Tupper Lake, which Hammond shot and killed. This sort of trigger-happy response shows well that bounties alone did not cause the demise of the large predators. Four years later, near Little Tupper Lake Hammond stayed up one night to hear wolves howling. On the same camping trip he claimed to have seen tracks of both wolves and mountain lions in the sand on the edge of Bog Lake.

Throughout the 1850s there were continued reports of wolves and mountain lions. One man wrote in 1897 that he had been prospecting for iron ore in the High Peaks in 1855. He declared, surely apocryphally, that he had been attacked by a pack of wolves after he had lost his way on a trail at night and that he fought them off for hours with a club and an axe. Finally, a companion came out looking for him with a dog, which managed to scare away the wolves still alive. A tall tale like this indicates how terrified of wolves people in the Adirondacks (and elsewhere) remained and what they were willing to believe.

In 1859 Benson Lossing wrote that mountain lions were almost extirpated in the Adirondacks and wolves were seldom seen except in winter. During the 1860s scattered sightings were reported around Raquette Lake, the Fulton Chain, and most of the central Adirondacks. In 1865 Moses Ames killed a mountain lion on the Saranac-Placid road, and two years later W. C. Robertson killed three at Long Lake. In 1868 A. B. Street identified what he was certain were mountain lion tracks at the foot of Mount Colden.

The state established bounties on wolves and mountain lions in 1871, intending to eliminate both species. The wolf and mountain lion were not long for the Adirondacks, but that the bounties alone were responsible for their extirpation is unlikely. Rather, survival simply became more and more difficult as their natural habitat was destroyed. Disease may also have been a factor, as distemper and rabies, introduced by domestic animals, spread to wild canids and cats. Mountain lions and wolves, by the end of the Civil War, were rare enough throughout the Adirondacks to deserve special notice whenever one was killed or sighted. A marginal farmer probably had more threats to his livelihood than just that presented by predators, but the loss of even one or two pigs or cows to a wolf could mean the difference between a family's comfort and real suffering.

The hatred and fear of predators was great enough for the settlers of the Adirondacks, as in nearly every other frontier part of the country, to demand that the state pay cash for them to be destroyed. A few stragglers of both species would persist in the Adirondacks until late in the nineteenth century, with a sighting or two even reported in the first years of the twentieth, but the fourth or fifth decade of the nineteenth saw the beginning of their decline toward extirpation.

* * *

The last story to be told of this era is the sad tale of the extirpation of the moose. By the 1850s the Adirondack moose was becoming noticeably scarce, and writers almost always accompanied mention of moose with a comment on its decline. C. Hart Merriam tracked down the last recorded sightings and killings of Adirondack moose. Except where otherwise noted, specific instances of moose being killed in the following account of the last days of the Adirondack moose are taken from his *The Mammals of the Adirondack Region*.

In 1851 John and Stevenson Constable killed two moose at the head of Independence Creek near Big Moose. The *History of Hamilton County* reports that the last moose in the town of Wells, probably the last native moose in the southern part of the county, was seen in 1852. In 1853 S. H. Hammond, who knew full well that moose were scarce in the Adirondacks, shot and killed on Rock Pond south of Little Tupper Lake the only live moose he had ever seen. Two guides, Alonzo Wood and Ed Arnold, killed two moose and found one dead behind Seventh Lake Mountain in 1853. In 1856 several moose were reported killed: an unnamed man shot one near Mud Lake near Lower Saranac. John and Stevenson Constable killed another moose at Charley's Pond in Hamilton County. Many years later John Constable expressed his regret to Merriam for having hastened the demise of the Adirondack moose: "I never recur to those hunts with any satisfaction, for much as I enjoyed at the time the tramp of more than a hundred miles on snow-shoes, the camping in the snow, the intense excitement of the search and pursuit, I must ever regret the part I have take unwittingly in exterminating this noble animal from our forests."

The last moose shot in the Saranac-Placid area was killed sometime between 1855 and 1858 by Truman Wilds on the road between Averyville and North Elba. Wilds was out hunting grouse with a double-barreled, muzzle-loading shotgun when he spotted a moose. He shot it directly in the face, blinded it with his first round, and then proceeded to fire off "a number of more shots at short range, finally fetching him down."

Sometime between 1854 and 1858, A. B. Street took a long trip up the Bog River to its headwaters. Only too aware of the moose's threatened status, he called this region "the deep, dark fastnesses which have now become the animal's haunt." That area and the country around Mount Seward and Indian Lake, according to Street, were then the only homes of "the almost mythic moose." Harvey Moody assured Street that only Mitchell Sabattis knew the woods around Seward well enough to track moose there. On Mud Lake, the source of the Bog River, Harvey Moody and Street went out jacking for a moose they believed they had heard from downstream. They found it, and Moody killed it with two shots. Street was led to ponder the rarity of the moose, "an animal uncommon even in this wild region, its existence scarce believed in by the denizens of our cities, and fast disappearing from these dark haunts, to live but in the traditions of the hunter's fireside." The possibility of protecting what was obviously an endangered species did not occur to him.

In 1858 a moose was seen but not shot near a garden on Raquette Lake. The next winter Horatio Seymour, a former governor of New York, killed a moose just north of Jock's Lake (now Honnedaga Lake) not far from West Canada Creek; this was probably the last moose killed in Herkimer County. The famous Raquette Lake guide Alvah Dunning is reported to have killed more than one moose somewhere along West Canada Creek in 1860.

Historian Alfred Donaldson strove mightily to give Dunning the dubious distinction of having shot the last Adirondack moose: "To be told that Alvah did not kill the last moose, is like being told that St. George did not kill the last dragon." Dunning was undoubtedly one of the great moose hunters of his day; he shot his first moose when he was eleven years old. For the next 35 years he made a living out of killing moose or leading others to where they could pull the trigger. In the early days, when he hunted moose with his father in southern Hamilton County, they often bagged three or four and sometimes as many as five a day. Fred Mather, a correspondent for *Forest and Stream* and other rod-and-gun journals of the late nineteenth century, wrote that Dunning was sure he remembered killing a moose in March of 1862, but no one else who investigated the issue — neither Merriam nor T. Madison Grant — could substantiate Dunning's claim.

In 1860 a group of Indians were seen heading up the Bog River on a moose-hunting expedition. The region at the source of the Bog River seems to have been generally recognized as one of the last strongholds of the Adirondack moose. From the accounts of the last moose killings it appears that they all occurred in the west central Adirondacks. If one drew a line around the area defined by the southern tip of Tupper Lake, the head of the Bog River, Thendara, and all of Raquette Lake, one would probably have enclosed the area where every moose except a few strays was killed or seen during the last decade of its existence in the Adirondacks.

The denouement in this story occurred in 1861. All the action centers at Raquette Lake, where the last three known native Adirondack moose were killed. In July of that year the artist A. F. Tait was camped with James B. Blossom on Raquette Lake. While they were there, Blossom killed a moose on the south inlet, and Tait wounded one on the Marion River. The moose wounded by Tait escaped into the forest but was killed early the next month by William Wood.

In the second week of August, 1861, the last moose was killed. A correspondent to *Forest and Stream*, Edward Clarence Smith, wrote in 1874 that he and a small group of men from Philadelphia and their guides had been fishing a few hundred yards upstream from the mouth of the Marion River. At about three o'clock they were returning to their camp on Raquette Lake when, rounding a turn in the river, they spied a large cow moose up to her rump in the water feeding on lily pads. The moose saw the boats and began slowly to make her way to the shore when one of the guides, Ed Palmer of Long Lake, leveled his rifle. Before he could shoot, the occupants of the other boat discharged several rounds of birdshot at the moose, but she took no notice. Palmer waited another minute or two and deliberately pulled his trigger. The moose shuddered and "fell heavily to rise no more." A companion of Smith's, Isaac Gerhart, later recalled, "We lived on her tenderloin—after getting her to camp under great difficulty—for about a week."

Harold K. Hochschild, in his *Township 34*, has written, "This question of who killed the last Adirondack moose has long been dangerous to ask. It has turned peaceful conversations into violent arguments, severed friendships, broken up happy marriages, and kept Adirondack historians in turmoil for the better part of a century." Yet Palmer's moose was indeed the last native moose recorded killed in the Adirondacks. Well into the 1870s, however, there were scattered reports of moose tracks throughout the area, but no substantive evidence of native moose in the Adirondacks after 1861 exists. Winslow C. Watson's *History of Essex County* implies that moose could still be found in Essex County as late as 1869. A correspondent to *Forest and Stream* in 1874 asserted that certain guides had recently seen moose tracks near Mud Pond, but the editor was doubtful. Verplanck Colvin, the great Adirondack surveyor, wrote that his guides identified moose tracks in the same area in the same year. In 1877 another correspondent to *Forest and Stream* wrote that moose tracks had been seen near Great Sand Lake, possibly what is now known as Sand Lake, near Woodhull Lake, in Herkimer County.

WILDLIFE AND THE WILDERNESS

By the 1850s the eastern moose, which a century earlier had occupied nearly all of New England as well as New York and much of Pennsylvania, had retreated to the Adirondacks and northern New England. After the last Adirondack moose died, the eastern moose persisted in Maine and northern Vermont and New Hampshire. Any moose sighted in the Adirondacks after the 1870s probably wandered in from the east or north. The 1877 report is the last tenuous claim for a vestigial population of Adirondack moose. Not long thereafter certain Adirondack landowners attempted to restock moose on private preserves, but there seems little doubt that the last native moose was gone certainly by the 1870s and probably by 1861. Of course, the last moose may not have been shot; it may simply have died somewhere in the deep woods. In any case, the passing of the moose marks a major watershed in the history of Adirondack wildlife.

The moose is a wilderness animal, able to live in a mature forest and threatened by the deer, which is favored by the changes that humans effect in a forest. The deer, which may have been at least partially responsible for the disappearance of the Adirondack moose, is an "edge" animal, living and multiplying in an environment altered by humans. The extirpation of the Adirondack moose suggests the end of wilderness in the Adirondacks, for it signifies the extent to which civilized activities had penetrated the depths of the North Woods. The emergence of the white-tailed deer as the principle Adirondack game species symbolizes the creation in the Adirondacks of a less wild environment, controlled by humans and exploited according to short-term needs.

In *The Maine Woods*, Thoreau wrote that sighting a moose was the climax and highest reward of a northeastern wilderness experience. He emphasized how moose truly belonged in the wilderness, and in a passage with special relevance to the Adirondacks speculated on the linguistic—in addition to the philosophical—importance of the moose. These marvelous creatures were, he wrote, "the true denizens of the forest, filling a vacuum which now first I discovered had not been filled for me—*Moose* men, *wood eaters*, the word is said to mean." The possibility that the word "moose" means "wood eater" is symbolically provocative. Most traditions explaining the origin and meaning of the word "Adirondack" hold that it signifies "bark eater" or "they who eat bark." If Thoreau is correct in his notion of the meaning of "moose," it suggests that, in a sense, moose were the original Adirondackers, the truly native species of a great wilderness. Before we can reasonably claim to have restored the condition of wilderness in the Adirondacks, we must guarantee the successful return of the region's most characteristic inhabitant.

5 Murray's Fools

IN THE SPRING OF 1869 the Boston publishing house of Fields, Osgood, & Co., released a volume entitled *Adventures in the Wilderness; or, Camp-Life in the Adirondacks* by the Reverend William Henry Harrison Murray. This immediately popular book found an eager readership and encouraged swarms of hunters, anglers, campers, and others to head for the Adirondacks. As "Wachusett," a correspondent to the *Boston Daily Advertiser*, observed,

> Mr. Murray's pen has brought a host of visitors into the Wilderness, such as it has never seen before — consumptives craving pure air, sportsmen hitherto content with small game and few fish . . . who threaten to turn the Wilderness into a Saratoga of fashionable costliness.

These neophyte sportsmen, quickly dubbed "Murray's Fools," became the subject of scores of articles, many humorous, in the Eastern press. The rush for the wilderness prompted by Murray, who for the rest of his checkered life was known as "Adirondack Murray," was a cultural phenomenon.

Before the Civil War the Adirondacks had been the treasured secret of a few, despite the popularity of books like Joel T. Headley's 1849 *The Adirondack; or, Life in the Woods*. After 1869, despite complaints from travelers whose experience in the wilderness was not quite as pleasant as they thought Murray promised it would be, camping and vacationing in the Adirondacks became fashionable. Not all of these people, of course, came for the sport, but many did. Murray himself was an avid hunter and fisherman, and many of the more seductive stories in his book are accounts of his exploits with the rod or gun. After 1869, the number of hunters aroused concern that Murray's Fools might actually kill off all the game and destroy the entire image of the Adirondacks as a place where genteel hunters pursued the well-established rituals of sport hunting.

Some of the woods and waterways, particularly popular lakes and rivers like the Fulton Chain and Raquette River, became crowded for the first time. In the summer of 1869 there was a shortage of guides, and many people complained of the lack of accommodations. Hotels soon popped up all over the Adirondacks. The conveniences of civilization appeared in the depths of the woods. As hotels and guides increased, so did the facility with which New Yorkers and other city folk could reach the central Adirondacks. Thomas C. Durant's railroad reached North Creek from Saratoga in 1871, and other lines soon penetrated the wilderness elsewhere. Regular stagecoach routes were established in the mid '70s. By 1878 steamboats were plying several Adirondack lakes.

The rush was on. Following Murray's lead, other writers issued guidebooks for every portion of the wilderness: Wallace's *Guide* was first issued in 1872 and Stoddard's in 1874. Both became popular references and were regularly updated and reprinted. According to hunters wistfully recalling the less crowded days before the Civil War, one could hardly visit any lake accessible by guideboat during the months of July and August without hearing throughout the day and night the cacophony of rifle shots and the shouts of hunters.

* * *

As before, the principle means of taking deer were jacking and hounding, and as more people tried one or the other, the debates over cruelty and sportsmanship became increasingly intense. Murray himself jacked many a deer, although he maintained that the most sporting of all types of hunting was done from shore during the day—what he called

> good, honest sport, and not slaughter, as when the dog drives a deer into the lake and, rowing up beside the poor frightened and struggling thing, the guide holds him by the tail while you blow his brains out. Bah! I should be ashamed to ever look along the sights of a rifle again if I had ever disgraced myself with any such "sporting" as that!

One of Murray's enemies tried to accuse him of breaking his own rules, asserting in an 1875 letter to *Forest and Stream*,

> The Rev. Dr. Wm. H. Murray has been at Cranberry Lake hounding deer since the middle of July. He has with him a large party, and it is to be regretted that he is permitted to annually enter this

state for the purpose of breaking the laws. It is said, even, that he has never killed a deer in season.

Killing deer out of season was a crime of which Murray and hundreds — if not thousands — of other Adirondack hunters were guilty. But as for the charge of hounding, E. T. Withmore, a friend of Murray's, wrote *Forest and Stream* a few weeks later to insist that Murray had never shot a hounded deer in his life and that all the Long Lake guides, who knew Murray well,

The Rush for the Wilderness. *Harper's Magazine*, 41 (1870).

would attest to his innocence on that count. Although Murray admitted that jacking was one of his favorite pastimes, he maintained that he seldom had the opportunity to practice it because he never killed more deer than he and his guide could eat. When he was alone in the woods with only one other man, he never shot more than one deer a week.

With the self-promotion that characterized his career, Murray claimed an invention (suggested by Headley twenty years earlier) that improved the torch-on-a-stick type of jacklight. With that kind of jack, the hunter could see only the sight at the end of the rifle and not the near sight on the his side of the light. Other disadvantages of the torch jack were its attractiveness to insects, the ease with which a light breeze might extinguish it, and its lack of maneuverability. Taking note of all these defects, Murray cut a hole in the top of a brimless fireman's helmet and attached a semi-cylindrical copper box with a round glass-covered opening on the flat side and reflec-

Murray's jack, from *Adventures in the Wilderness* (1869)

tors facing the opening. Through the hole the hunter inserted a candle and, donning the hat, would be wearing something similar to a miner's helmet, directing the light whichever way he turned his head. Now he had maneuverability never afforded by a torch-style jacklight and could also see the near sight of his rifle.

The problem of sights had already been solved by most jackers, though in a perhaps unimaginative manner: they simply used a shotgun instead of a rifle. Unable to see the forward sight they pointed their shotgun in the general direction of the deer and blasted away. Murray disdained the use of a shotgun in hunting deer but came up with his own efficient improvement on the jacklight. In any event, the deer was killed by an unseen hunter from behind an inexplicable and hypnotizing light. C. Hart Merriam acridly declared that jacking was like "carrying a lantern, any dark night, through a frontier pasture, and shooting the first unlucky cow that chances to stand in the path."

A particularly controversial practice, apparently more and more employed by market hunters, was crusting in the months of February and March when alternating freezes and thaws had built up a hard crust on the snow. This crust was often hard enough to support men on snowshoes but not the sharp hoofs of deer. Hunters on snowshoes would find a place where deer had yarded up for the winter and kill them at will. Since venison was difficult to get out of the woods when deep snow was on the ground, a great number of the deer that were killed by crusting were skinned and left to rot in the forest. The skins alone made the expedition worthwhile, and the hunter did not have to lug out the heavy meat.

The hunting method that was probably the most sporting, though it too was certainly not without its critics and detractors, was still-hunting, which meant to most writers either waiting for deer at a stationary point or tracking them in the snow. In either case, the hunter worked without the assistance of hounds or lights. In the Adirondacks the first snow often falls in October when the bucks are fat and the antlers are in their finest condition. Still-hunting calls for stamina and woodcraft, and, oddly, this was one of the main criticisms of it as a sport. Its opponents maintained that still-hunting was viable only for the strong and experienced. Carrying the logic of democracy to an absurd extreme, they argued that every man, no matter how out of shape or ignorant of the ways of the forest, had a right to bag a deer, and still-hunting, as its adherents desired, should thus never be made the only legal means of killing deer in New York. (This argument suggests the equally ludicrous claim that designating any publicly owned land as wilderness and restricting motorized access is undemocratic because the handicapped or the infirm will not be able to visit it.)

A variation of still-hunting involved setting out a salt lick and waiting to shoot the deer that were attracted to it. Salt licks, prohibited by law as early as 1871, were employed widely for many years and are still occasionally found. Hunters who used hounds condemned the placement of salt licks and still-hunting in general, as well as jacking, because they were quiet and therefore appeared sneaky and unsporting.

A. F. Tait, "Still Hunting on the First Snow: A Second Shot" (1855).
(Collection Adirondack Museum)

* * *

A complicating factor in all the debates over the proper way to hunt was feuding between city sports and Adirondack natives, each group accusing the other of depleting the deer herd. Jacking, most practicable in the summer by vacationing city sportsmen, was defended by downstate hunters. Hounding and crusting, most often occurring in the fall and winter, were naturally defended by year-round residents. The large hotels, the proprietors of most of which wanted the state to maintain a laissez-faire posture, fought all forms of protective legislation for years. As a result, New York was one of the last states in the East permanently to prohibit both jacking and hounding at all times of the year.

As for the continuing debate over the virtues and vices of jacking, more than one observer pointed out that during the summer shooting deer by any means was illegal and that all the opponents of jacking needed to do was see that the laws already on the books were enforced. Enforcing the game laws was extremely difficult, however. Deer hunting was an incredibly sensitive issue—as it still is—and enforcing the law often meant that whoever was doing the enforcing was sending a neighbor to jail. Too many Adirondack hunters—both native and downstate—did not want statutory regulation. As long as there were substantial numbers of hunters who wanted to jack deer in June, there was no law that could stop them.

Before Murray's *Adventures in the Wilderness*, the disputes among Adirondack hunters revolved around definitions of sportsmanship and virility. After Murray the arguments often depended on the premise that the Adirondack deer herd was declining and that whatever method for bagging deer one did not happen to employ himself was responsible for the decline. (In fact, although by 1880 deer were practically extirpated throughout New York State except in the Adirondacks, the northern herd continued to grow as lumbering and forest fires steadily furnished it with more and more habitat.) The arguments seldom considered what might be best for the deer. Few of the pleas to the legislature for changes in the game laws were predicated on a love for nature, a wish to keep deer around because by that time they were an established part of the Adirondack ecology, or even a sense that they were picturesque. The essence of each side's position was that a healthy deer population was a profitable and useful facet of the Adirondack environment and that the state should not let this valuable asset be destroyed.

The image of the white-tailed deer as a merchantable commodity was in the Adirondacks to stay and has established itself more firmly as the years have passed. In the eighties and nineties the debate reached new levels of intensity. *Forest and Stream*, founded in 1873 and quickly the premier American journal devoted to field sports, became one of the main forums for the interminable accusations and recriminations hurled back and forth among the various camps. In these verbal wars, the rhetoric was consistently melodramatic and the putative stakes enormous. With glacial ponderousness, the state did manage gradually to assert control over what was happening, in the name of sport or profit, to the deer in the Adirondacks. The establishment of control over the game in the Adirondacks paralleled the establishment of control over the land itself and its timber and water. Inexorably, game laws (to be discussed in the next chapter) reached the Adirondacks.

* * *

Behind much of the fury over game laws and concern over the ostensible decline in the deer herd lay the suspicion of many sportsmen that *their* private domain was being invaded by the wrong sort of people. This fear largely stemmed from the conviction that deer hunting was historically and properly the pursuit of aristocrats. Beneath the inflated prose of many of the articles arguing the merits or demerits of one or another form of hunting was the assumption that Adirondack deer by rights belonged to a certain class and that the efforts of others to join in the sport were vulgar, offensive, and often laughable. This assumption reflected the persistence in at least part of American culture of European values. In Europe, wildlife is generally not owned by the state but by the title holder of the land where it is found. And in Europe, hunting has traditionally been a sport for the landed gentry. Peasants did not hunt for sport, although of course they often hunted (or poached) for survival. Many Americans, despite their seeming dedication to egalitarian ways, wanted to impose the European model on hunting and on determining who should hunt.

In 1870, Charles Hallock, a well known outdoor writer, who a few years later became the first editor of *Forest and Stream*, wrote a typical account of the arrivistes. In a satirical attack on Murray's Fools published in *Harper's Monthly*, Hallock described the fictional exploits of four characteristic "fools" of the summer of 1869. Devoured by black flies, they ran into hundreds of other campers everywhere they turned, wandered desultorily along the Raquette River route, and generally made idiots of themselves in their efforts to hunt and fish. Hallock's point was how out of place these men were and how their very presence diminished the wilderness experience of others.

Similar accounts of the escapades of novices in the Adirondacks—either humorous or openly hostile—filled the columns of *Forest and Stream* for the rest of the century. In 1880 one of *Forest and Stream*'s most popular and most articulate contributors, George Washington Sears, who wrote under the pen-name "Nessmuk," canoed through the Fulton Chain-Raquette Lake country and, among other things, reported on the crowds of incompetent hunters and fishermen he encountered: "Every tourist had his breech-loading battery, and a full supply of rods, reels, and lines, which is a great comfort to the average tourist and does small damage to trout and deer." Fred Mather, another popular outdoor writer of the day, expressed the proprietary resentment that many sportsmen felt toward the newcomers:

> I would readily fall into sympathy with the men who have visited the woods for the past thirty or forty years, and who have come

from a love of the vast solitudes which railroads and good wagon roads are now rendering too easy of access to the ordinary tourist, and who are finding that the charms of *their* woods are gone.

With its italicized possessive this passage makes only too clear the sense of prior right to the Adirondacks which some sportsmen felt. An 1888 editorial in *Forest and Stream*, "Adirondack Abominations," echoed this sentiment: "Between the fish-hog, the railroad, the Italian railroad hand, the night-hunter, the pseudo-sportsman and the like, this grand region is becoming yearly less and less like its old self and a few more more years will witness its entire destruction from a sportsman's and nature-lover's point of view."

The condescension which the self-anointed true sportsmen evinced toward those who were still discovering the pleasures of camping and field sports evolved into the perception that the newcomers were destroying the Adirondack deer herd. Behind the endless debate about deer laws was the assumption that hunters could be divided into two classes: one class was aware of certain gentlemanly traditions of sportsmanship and humanity, and the other was composed of a mob of blood-thirsty butchers, who indiscriminately slaughtered does and fawns. The tales related by the right people about the wrong people were gory and convincing: one correspondent to *Forest and Stream* wrote that three men from Syracuse had camped at Gull Pond in Herkimer County and had killed twenty-three deer in six weeks, leaving most of the meat to rot. Similar horror stories appeared in *Forest and Stream* throughout this period.

* * *

The inevitable result of the fear that sport hunting might be destroyed by inept intruders was the ultimate manifestation of the elite, proprietary impulse — the private game preserve. The English tradition of aristocratically owned and protected game preserves partially explains why some sportsmen wished to own large tracts of Adirondack land. The more important explanation for this phenomenon, which took sudden and ominous shape late in the nineteenth century, is the perception that the old days in the Adirondacks were threatened and that those hunters and fishermen who wanted to save the gentlemanly sporting arts would have to do it on their own property. Before the establishment of these private preserves, large Adirondack holdings had mostly been the property of commercial interests — iron mines, lumber companies, or railroads. In nearly every case field sports had been pursued whenever and wherever they did not interfere with the economic exploitation of the land.

After the beginning of the Murray era, however, some owners of Adirondack land saw the possibility and inferred the need of identifying their holdings as game preserves. At first these preserves were enthusiastically supported by the sporting press, which believed that anything which forestalled the anticipated extirpation of the Adirondack deer was a step in the right direction. Thus *Forest and Stream* approvingly reported in 1878 that the proprietors of the Adirondack Railroad were planning to establish a park of a million acres to protect game and fish. Later, this trend was seen as a threat to the average sportsman. In its consideration of what these private holdings meant for the future of the Adirondacks, *Forest and Stream* found itself addressing a tricky situation. For years that journal had promulgated the elitist response to Murray's Fools, representing the position of sportsmen who detested the inexperienced hunter and anyone else not properly imbued with the traditions of Adirondack sportsmanship.

But in the establishment of private game preserves, which simply represented the logical next step in the elitist position, *Forest and Stream* discovered a threat to field sports more sinister than that posed by the greenest novice. Having fostered a climate which led to the removal of large portions of its own favorite wilderness from the reach of its faithful readers, *Forest and Stream* was now forced to shift its stance and attack the large preserves as undemocratic. Fearing that a few wealthy men would soon own all the prime hunting and fishing lands in the Adirondacks, the editors adopted the defense of the common sportsman, whose right to recreation appeared impinged by a few land-hungry plutocrats.

One of the chief objects of this fear was the Adirondack League Club, founded by New York City and western New York sportsmen in 1890 and controlling a massive preserve of over 125,000 acres near Old Forge. The League Club was well aware of the value of its lands and noted in its 1891 yearbook, "We have an absolute and indefeasible title to the most valuable tract in the Adirondacks, whether regarded as a productive forest or as a magnificent sporting preserve."

The club's exclusivity, shared by many of the other clubs of the day, was well illustrated in the same yearbook, where the officers invited nominations — to be sent to an office on Wall Street — of new members, promising "that the present high character of the membership [will] be maintained." Once nominated, a prospective member had to pass "practically unanimous election by the Board of Trustees, so carefully is the membership guarded against undesirable or uncongenial associates." The following year the officers repeated their commitment to "exclude every candidate whose character, reputation, or habits might tend to make him uncongenial in the slightest degree to any other member." In the racially charged atmosphere of the late nineteenth century, these were thinly disguised warnings against all non-Anglo Saxons, especially Jews.

In 1891 *Forest and Stream* editorialized, "The private fishing club and the exclusive game preserve are devouring the Adirondacks. Vast tracts are passing into their control; their trespass signs multiply with the years." Correspondents to the journal picked up this theme and argued that the large private holdings threatened to push the average sportsman out of the Adirondacks altogether. One man wrote, "Syndicates are working together with the ultimate purpose of bringing the entire region under private ownership by men of great wealth. The Indians were driven out long ago, and now the humble sportsman must soon go." Finally, the editors, citing mainly the Adirondack League Club and Dr. W. Seward Webb's Nehasane Park, concluded that "the heart of the region, so to speak, has been cut out and appropriated by private interests."

There were many other such preserves, and eventually the state became equally concerned about this problem. In the *Annual Report* of the Forest, Fish and Game Commission released in 1904, the Commissioners noted the enmity stirred up between preserve owners and those locked out:

> The comparatively sudden exclusion of the public from its old camping grounds has provoked a bitter hostility on the part of the hunters, fishermen and guides who formerly ranged over this territory. The sportsman who returns to some favorite haunt only to find himself confronted with the words, "No thoroughfare," turns back with a resentful feeling, while the guides, who were wont to conduct their patrons wherever game was plentiful, view with threatening looks the hired game-keepers that guard the forbidden lands.

Many of the large game preserves exist today, and it is common knowledge that the deer hunting on private land, where the forest is managed, is superior to that on the state-owned Forest Preserve, where the forever-wild provision of the State Constitution prohibits any interference in the forest environment, including wildlife habitat improvement. But in an interesting twist in public opinion and perception, the large preserves are not viewed with much antipathy by those hunters who are barred from hunting on them.

* * *

C. Hart Merriam, a downstate medical doctor, dropped his practice in order to have more time to pursue his true interest, zoology. For many years he researched the mammals of the Adirondacks and read what he called their "biographies" to meetings of the New York Linnæan Society. These life stories were collated and published in the Society's *Transactions*. In 1884 they were republished, unchanged, as *The Mammals of the Adirondack Region*. At the time, Merriam's work was the only comprehensive scientific work on Adirondack mammals and the first effort to summarize their status since James DeKay's *Zoology of New York* of the 1840s.

By 1882 the mountain lion, pressed by bounties and loss of habitat, was rare and approaching extirpation. A law establishing bounties on the large Adirondack predators was passed on April 26, 1871, and read, in part, as follows: "A State bounty of thirty dollars for a grown wolf, fifteen dollars for a pup wolf, and twenty dollars for a panther, shall be paid to any person or persons who shall kill any of said animals within the boundaries of this State." The first payment for an Adirondack mountain lion under this law was made to Spencer Ward of the town of Fine in St. Lawrence County for a mountain lion killed on June 7, 1871. Over the next eleven years (through August 1882) the state paid bounties on forty-six mountain lions, five of which were killed in Essex County, two in Franklin, three in Hamilton, five in Herkimer, four in Lewis, and twenty-seven in St. Lawrence. Merriam researched the records of mountain lions killed in the Adirondacks prior to the establishment of the state bounty and reckoned from the available data that between 1860 and 1882 approximately one hundred mountain lions were killed in Adirondack counties.

One of these was shot by Verplanck Colvin near a deer yard on Seventh Lake Mountain on February 15, 1877. This animal weighed about two hundred pounds, was the largest mountain lion known to have been killed in the state of New York, and ranks among the largest mountain lions ever killed in North America. After Colvin's guides had dragged the carcass around the woods with him for several days, Colvin took it to Albany where it was stuffed and mounted and then placed in the rotunda of the state house for viewing by the legislature. According to Merriam, Colvin did not collect the state bounty.

The wolf was also becoming rare: "Comparatively few wolves are now to be found in the Adirondacks," wrote Merriam, "though twelve years ago they were quite abundant, and used to hunt in packs of half a dozen or more." Between 1871 and 1882 the state paid bounties on only forty-five wolves — not nearly enough, according to Merriam, to account for the sudden decrease from the time when they had been so common that "scarcely a night passed when they could not be heard howling in various parts of the forest." The reason for this decline was probably not so much the bounty as the destruction of the wolf's natural habitat by logging and other forest-clearing activities. The wolf is a particularly wilderness-oriented animal and cannot tolerate interference in its environment. It is also subject to a variety of diseases, such as rabies and distemper, that it can acquire from domestic animals.

For the wolf, as with the mountain lion, the greater number by far of the state bounties were paid in St. Lawrence County, where thirty-one wolves were killed. In addition, two each were killed in Essex, Herkimer, Lewis, and Washington counties and three in Franklin and Oneida. Of the thirty-one wolves for which bounties were paid in St. Lawrence County, George Muir of the town of Fine killed fourteen; the same man collected bounties on fifteen mountain lions. In twenty-one years George Muir made $705 from the state alone (one of the wolves he killed was a pup and therefore worth only fifteen dollars) for killing wolves and mountain lions — more money than any other man made from bounties in the same period. Of course, Muir and other bounty hunters may have been showing the same carcasses to different town clerks and collecting double or triple bounties for one animal. This has been a common practise wherever bounties have been used.

The remaining predator populations were also declining. The wolverine had been extirpated. The bobcat and lynx were considered rare. The fox was being persecuted unmercifully but was holding its own. The fisher population had declined substantially, but Merriam believed that it was not in danger of extirpation. Of the fur bearers only the beaver was seriously threatened, and it was so rare that many people believed it no longer existed in New York. During the fall of 1880 a beaver was caught on the Raquette near Axton. Merriam himself later examined the area and saw signs of at least one other beaver. The only other beavers he knew of in the Adirondacks were one colony in the wilderness around the headwaters of the West Branch of the St. Regis River. Outdoor writer Harry Radford estimated that the Adirondack beaver population in 1880 was not more than twenty-five individuals and that every one of them was in Township 20 in the southern part of the town of Santa Clara in Franklin County. This included the northern edge of Upper Saranac Lake and the small ponds and streams around St. Regis Pond and Lake Clear.

Marten remained relatively common and were trapped by the hundreds every year. Ermine, mink, otter, and muskrat also remained abundant enough to withstand continued trapping. Merriam distinguished numerous species of smaller, commercially unimportant mammals, all of which seemed to be thriving in the Adirondacks despite the destruction of a large part of their habitat. Among these were three species of moles, three of shrews, five of bats, six of squirrels, six of rats and mice, and three of hares and rabbits. (Merriam's taxonomy is no longer current.)

Culver H. Lewis, " An Adirondack Episode — Taking Possession of the Camp," Frank Leslie's Illustrated Newspaper, 14 July 1883.
(Collection Adirondack Museum)

Bear, since the extirpation of the moose the largest animal in the Adirondack forest, continued to thrive although they were always shot on sight. Around the farms in the Lake Champlain Valley many farmers complained that they were losing substantial numbers of sheep and other livestock to bear predation. Although there was no state bounty at this time, Essex County had one, but it is doubtful that it contributed to any decline in their numbers. Bear were commonly thought of as disagreeable, useless, and unpalatable. Because of their size they were occasionally sought by hunters for trophies, but they were never considered legitimate game animals in the same way that deer were, although some hunters did insist that bear meat, killed at the right time of year and prepared properly, was tasty.

Merriam described the passing of the moose and observed the amazing (to him) abundance of deer in the Adirondacks despite the fact that "during the present century hundreds of them have perished of cold and starvation, hundreds have been killed by wolves and mountain lions, and thousands by their natural enemy man." The reason that deer continued to increase in the Adirondacks throughout the nineteenth century, despite the fact that the Adirondacks do not provide the deer with an adequate range, was, as we have seen, the extensive lumbering operations that opened up one part of the wilderness after another to forest fires and new growth. Because of logging, all over the Adirondacks, in all types of forest and terrain, there was a continual change in the character of the forest.

6 Limits and Seasons

AS HUNTING IN THE ADIRONDACKS became increasingly popular, the legislature began to scrutinize the state's game laws. Until the mid-nineteenth century, as we have seen, the only law governing hunting was a 1788 statute prohibiting killing deer before August 1 or after December 31 and proscribing the use of hounds. Routinely ignored, this law for nearly seventy years stood as the sole statute regarding deer hunting throughout the state. The alacrity with which writers of the Headley era published accounts clearly describing violations suggests that few Adirondack hunters were concerned about it. Despite, or perhaps because of, this climate of resistance to game laws, the New York legislature, beginning around 1860, spent nearly half a century passing, revising, and cancelling a series of statutes governing seasons, limits, and methods for hunting; throughout, the chief focus was deer hunting. Opposition to these efforts was often bitter, but by about 1910 the legislature had achieved reasonable control, although in the Adirondacks, as in all rural parts of the country, some illegal hunting has persisted.

The two main issues were dates for open season and how deer could be legally hunted. In either case, class and regional antagonisms constituted a major part of the debate. Downstate sport hunters—often affluent, professional men—wanted hunting to be legal in the summer, and they wanted no prohibitions on jacking—which was primarily a summer activity. At the same time, they sought restrictions on any type of hunting occurring during the fall, winter, or spring, and they particularly lobbied for a prohibition on hounding, which came to be associated with fall hunting by local residents who sold venison to hotels and restaurants. The locals worked to protect hounding and began to see all summer shooting, especially jacking, as the sport of wealthy tourists. The legislature was pressed on every side.

Should deer be understood and thus protected as trophies for summer sportsmen? Or did they naturally belong to the locals to be used for food and commerce?

Deer lobbies proliferated. As soon as one party got what it wanted, its opponents went to work for repeal. Often they succeeded, and the original lobby returned to Albany, pressuring the next legislature. Laws were passed against hounding on five different occasions, but the first four were repealed by legislatures sensitive to North-Country leverage. By 1907 *Forest and Stream* could report that hounding, jacking, night shooting, and all killing of deer in water were illegal, but the steps culminating in those statutory prohibitions were contested at nearly every point.

* * *

In 1857 the legislature restated the dates for the open season and included the important provision that possession of venison or green hides during the closed season was evidence of having illegally taken a deer. Though not immediately useful, the connection between possession and presumed guilt eventually became the major tool of game wardens in their efforts to discover and prosecute game-law violations. Without it, game wardens had to catch every violator in the act — an impossibility in the Adirondacks. Two years later, all previous game laws were repealed; this made hounding legal again.

The next important amendment to the game laws occurred in 1867 when the deer season was opened on October 1. Pushing the opening date for deer season into the autumn doubtless angered many of the summer sportsmen who came to the Adirondacks for jacking. But the following year the opening date was returned to August 1, and the closing date was set at December 10. In 1869 the open-season dates were again changed (to August 15 and December 31). More important, the law of 1869 prohibited hounding at all times throughout the state — an indication that summer jackers had found a friendly ear in Albany. People who lived in the Adirondacks interpreted such a maneuver as a threat to their right to make a living.

In 1871 the opening day of the season was again moved to August 1, and the prohibition on hounding was limited to that part of the state north of the Mohawk River. This provision may have pacified hounders on Long Island, but it left the Adirondack native as disgruntled as ever. Not only was hounding still illegal in the Adirondacks, but dogs illegally in pursuit of deer could be killed by anyone who saw them. A further stipulation of the 1871 law was the provision that county boards of supervisors could authorize the towns in their county to elect game constables to be paid by the town. The use of salt licks, traps, and "spring guns" was also declared illegal.

North Country legislators did not abandon their constituents, however. In 1872 they pushed through a bill moving the opening date to September 1 — a direct affront to summer jackers — and legalized hounding throughout the state except in Steuben County. The closing date of the deer season was set at November 10. Two years later, the closing date was reset at November 30. With all these changes of opening and closing dates one should not imagine that hunters in the Adirondacks waited anxiously to see what the legislature would do next with the deer season. The official dates remained unimportant to most hunters. As "P. H. A." reported to *Forest and Stream* in 1873, "here [in the Adirondacks] every man is a law unto himself, and nobody thinks of prosecuting an offender against the laws of the State."

* * *

It was to combat just that indifference to the laws that the New York Association for the Protection of Game was established in 1874. Its parent organization was the New York Sportsman's Club, founded in 1844 by socially prominent New York City sportsmen. Originally its membership had been limited to one hundred of the city's elite, but by the time it was re-organized as the New York Association for the Protection of Game, its rolls were enlarged, although it remained aristocratic. One of its first measures was an attempt to convince New York high society, accustomed to stylish dining on all sorts of game throughout the year, that serving game out of season was bad form.

In another step, the Association set aside money from its treasury to pay for the private enforcement of the game laws. In 1869, $1000 was appropriated for paying detectives and informers, and in 1874 members designated $2500 to pay detectives, make rewards, and finance the prosecution of game-law offenses. Among other things, the Association hired detectives to raid New York City game dealers and search for illegally held meat. The Association believed that if the state's deer herd was declining, market hunters must be responsible. At the same time, however, the hunters who lived and made a living in the North Country persisted in their accusations that it was these very sportsmen, with their jacking and summer shooting, who were killing all the deer.

* * *

In 1877 hounding was abolished again. Throughout the mid seventies *Forest and Stream* waged a relentless editorial campaign against the killing of deer in the Adirondacks by local people during the fall. Assuming that downstate hunters had some sort of proprietary right to Adirondack deer, the editors lobbied zealously for anti-hounding legislation. Arguing that the locals killed more deer in the fall than all the sportsmen put together in the summer, *Forest and Stream* (whose readership, one must assume, was mostly among the sportsman class, and not among the guides) called for special restrictions on hounding and for officers paid by the state to enforce the law.

In Charles Fenton, owner of the hotel at Number Four in Lewis County, the downstate summer hunters found a welcome ally. He wrote often and eloquently to *Forest and Stream* about the thousands of deer that he maintained were being slaughtered by locals using hounds in the autumn. In 1875 he asserted that for every deer killed by a sportsman in the summer four were killed before the hounds in the fall. He declared that he personally knew of many parties that killed over twenty deer apiece before hounds and demanded that the legislature at least prohibit hounding after October 15.

Through 1875 and 1876, many correspondents wrote to *Forest and Stream* to express their sympathy with anti-hounding editorials. One man declared that he thought jacking was just as difficult as stalking or still-hunting and asked the editors for their opinion; predictably, the editors concurred. Throughout this anti-hounding battle, *Forest and Stream* purveyed one story after another about summer jacking as a legitimate and ostensibly uncontroversial sport. In one eerie account, a correspondent identifying himself as "Tahawus" jacked a deer and returned to his campsite, where he and his guide broiled and ate the heart for a midnight snack.

The next target of *Forest and Stream* was "still hunters," by which *Forest and Stream* meant winter hunting to supply logging camps. The editors reported in 1878, "There has been much complaint recently of the operations of still hunters in the Adirondacks. Great numbers of deer have been slaughtered in the 'yards.'" As soon as the editorial identified "still hunters" as villainous, every hunter in the Adirondacks who stalked deer in the autumn rose up to defend his sport. For the next few years the magazine was filled by accusations that still hunters were slaughtering deer in March followed by the arguments of the still hunters that the men who killed deer in winter were not still hunters at all but were pot or market hunters. In this confusion, the editorial steam, which had demonstrated again that the sport hunting faction saw any market hunting by locals as suspect and in need of prohibition, dissipated.

Meanwhile, the defenders of hounding were hard at work — both in the woods, where they had never stopped hounding, and in Albany, where they relentlessly worked to have the 1877 anti-hounding law repealed. Reporting on the uselessness of that law, Charles Fenton wrote in late November of 1878 that 150 deer had been killed that year near Smith's Lake by hunters using hounds. Throughout the Adirondacks, Fenton insisted, thousands of deer had been slaughtered before hounds by guides, hotel owners, and local hunters.

In 1879 pro-hounding sentiment prevailed, and the 1877 law was repealed, with the restriction that hounding was permitted only between August 15 and November 1 and not at all in St. Lawrence County. In addition, the opening date of the deer season, for the first time in eight years, was returned to August 1. As before, the official dates for opening and closing the deer season seem not to have impressed most hunters. In 1878 the Long Lake Club, an organization of local guides, was established and announced, at a time when it was still illegal to kill deer before the first of September, that no deer were to be shot in their district before July 10. Hunters, by and large, went about their accustomed routines as if nothing were happening.

* * *

An occasional prosecution did take place, but when the offenders were tried in their own or neighboring towns, there was little chance of a stiff sentence. In July of 1879 a man and his two sons went into the Chateaugay Lakes and killed forty deer in ten days. Taking only the skins, they left the carcasses to rot in the woods. A local prosecutor brought the men to trial, where they were fined a total of forty dollars. Lamenting this apparent failure of the system, one writer in *Forest and Stream* suggested that a more appropriate penalty would have been for the offenders to be forced back into the woods to eat the rancid meat.

Gradually, those concerned about legal sport in the Adirondacks concluded that the problem was not so much the lack of proper legislation as the near total absence of enforcement of existing laws. One cynical observer wrote in 1880:

> Game laws are here a mere laughing stock; nobody regards them, for the reason that they are seldom or never enforced; and because the poor natives here depend on game for all the fresh meat they ever eat, all the year round. Sportsmen and campers must take fish, partridge and deer during their summer vacations, or live on salt pork and canned meats.

LIMITS AND SEASONS

The downstate clubs like the New York Association for the Protection of Game were saying that if there was to be game tomorrow, there must be restraint today. But they asked only the locals and market hunters to exercise this restraint. The Adirondack natives were saying that they knew what they were doing was illegal but everybody did it. If they stopped, all they would get would be empty stomachs and empty wallets. The average vacationing hunter was not saying anything or listening to anybody. He killed a deer wherever, whenever, and however he chose. And he never had any problem in securing a guide: if a law-abiding guide refused him, there was always someone else.

In editorial after editorial, *Forest and Stream* called for the establishment of a State Game Association to oversee a single, operative, adequate game law. Despairing of state enforcement, the editors turned to wealthy sportsmen to organize themselves into a vigilante organization. This approach depended on the old premise that all hunting for sport was gentlemanly and therefore legitimate: it was the men who hunted for profit and supplied the restaurants and hotels in the cities who were really diminishing the Adirondack deer herd. As *Forest and Stream* opined in 1880,

> Fish mongers and game dealers, grasping for the almighty dollar, serve as go-betweens for the restaurant keeper and the hotel proprietor, and shield the nefarious deeds of the pot hunter behind their guise of respectability and their moneyed weight. It requires vigilance to catch the skulking game thief, and it requires nerve to attack the law-defying marketmen.

No doubt many deer were killed by market hunters, but it was naive and inconsistent for *Forest and Stream* to attack only them while it routinely and approvingly published accounts of city sportsmen illegally shooting deer — many of them does — in July.

In 1880 the legislature responded, tentatively, in the direction of enforcement, providing for the appointment of eight game protectors for the entire state. Of these eight, two were to cover the Adirondacks — Sylvester J. Palmer of Indian Lake and John Liberty of Elizabethtown. These appointments were little more than a gesture. How could two men be expected to discover and prevent or prosecute infractions of the law in an area as large as the state of Massachusetts?

Despite the intimidating demands of this mandate, *Forest and Stream* reported that Palmer was enforcing the game laws strictly in the Indian Lake area, keeping out-of-season venison and trout out of the hotels, patrolling the woods on snowshoes, and searching for incidents of crusting.

But that was only one region, and even though the legislature doubled the number of Game Protectors in 1883, it would be many years before the combination of enough wardens and public cooperation would significantly diminish illegal hunting in the Adirondacks.

* * *

Meanwhile, the debate over how to hunt continued. *Forest and Stream* finally began to realize that perhaps it was not the market hunters alone who were killing deer in the Adirondacks. In 1881 the editors suggested that jackers save themselves the trouble of traveling to the Adirondacks or Michigan by going to the local slaughterhouses and shooting pigs and cattle. Perhaps one reason why *Forest and Stream* began to criticize jacking was that local Adirondack hunters had reportedly returned to this practice. Correspondent "Adrian Ondack" claimed that local people were jacking in June just for fun and were killing as many as four deer a night.

The hotels, which probably thrived on the controversy because it announced that illegal hunting was universally practiced and accepted in the Adirondacks, managed to keep venison on their tables throughout June and July. "Hardy" suggested to *Forest and Stream* that the game protection associations post men at all the hotels in the Adirondacks to see that guides that hunted for table venison were arrested and to prevent sportsmen from shooting before August 1.

Hounding was increasingly criticized. Although jacking was evidently in disfavor in the *Forest and Stream* editorial offices, hounding remained the chief target. Late in 1884 the journal solicited opinions on hounding. Predictably, most readers were opposed, as were the editors, who also provided petition forms, calling for a ban on hounding, to be filled out and mailed to legislators. An intensive campaign was begun to lobby the 1885 session of the New York Legislature for an anti-hounding law. On January 15, 1885, a typical editorial began,

> It is pretty well understood that the hounding of deer, as practiced in the Adirondacks, is destructive, unsportsmanlike and brutal. And it is high time that it were abolished. Visiting sportsmen and Adirondack residents are agreed on that point.

On June 13 of that year the legislature passed a law forbidding hounding anywhere in the state except Suffolk County. *Forest and Stream* was forced to acknowledge strenuous opposition from residents of towns on the Adirondack periphery.

As soon as the anti-hounding bill was passed, the pro-hounding forces again mobilized their legions and prepared to descend on the 1886 legislative session. In New York City, fifty game dealers joined in opposition to the anti-hounding law, asserting that New York State based its laws on the demands of summer shooting dudes rather than on either common sense or the needs of the people who actually lived in the Adirondacks. "W. C. W." wrote *Forest and Stream* to suggest that jacking should also be made illegal to assure Adirondack natives that the laws were not directed against them alone. Local people indeed did think that they stood no chance against the power of downstate interests. They owned the dogs, and they used them. But a law had been passed against them in favor of hunters who came to the Adirondacks from outside the area, who did not hunt with hounds, but who could be seen jacking deer on every lake and river from July to September.

With the weight of the New York City game dealers behind them, North Country legislators pushed through a repeal of the anti-hounding law, but the 1886 law contained a novel provision that would eventually put the game market out of business. For the first time, hunters were limited in the number of deer they could kill. Each hunter was permitted to kill three deer and no more. At the time, the 1886 law was revolutionary. For years hunters and legislators had been arguing over when a hunter could shoot deer and in what manner, but no one had thought to tell him how many.

As in the 1879 repeal, the 1886 law carried the provision that hounding remained illegal in St. Lawrence County and that in those counties where it was legal it was restricted—in this case to between September 1 and October 5. Again, dogs illegally in pursuit of deer could be shot on sight. The opening and closing dates for the entire season were changed to August 15 and November 1, thus closing the season at an earlier date than at any time in New York history. The early closing no doubt reflected an effort to prevent entirely putatively destructive winter hunting.

Forest and Stream, meanwhile, was not unaware that an anti-jacking measure would to some degree mollify the North Country antipathy to city sportsmen and city-oriented lobbying. In 1883 it came out explicitly against jacking, declaring that although it was most often done during the closed season and was therefore virtually illegal anyway, it should be specifically prohibited. The whole notion of summer shooting began to receive special treatment from *Forest and Stream*, as the editors concluded that killing deer in the summer was perhaps the most unsporting kind of hunting practiced in the Adirondacks. As the campaign advanced, it became feverish. One maudlin editorial described a man awakened in the middle of the night by a spirit that carried him to an Adirondack lake, where he was shown the emaciated bodies of two fawns. On his return he was told that the spirit was the mother of the fawns and that she had been killed while they were still nursing.

In 1888 the legislature passed a new deer law with no difference from the old except to permit hounding for fifteen more days, until October 20. The opening and closing dates, August 15 and November 1, remained the same. Among hotel owners, at least around Utica and Boonville, there was considerable sentiment for again extending the opening of the season to the first of August. In 1893 the legislature extended the legal time for hounding to between September 10 and October 10. Crusting was declared illegal again — an indication that it was still practiced relatively widely.

In 1892 the number of game protectors for the state was increased from sixteen to twenty, still woefully short of a force large enough to have any real effect on the illegal hunting persisting throughout the Adirondacks. Now and then a man would be arrested and sometimes tried for offenses under the game law, but convictions were rare. In 1895 the famous Adirondack French Louie, who lived the life of a semi-hermit at West Canada Lake, was arrested for killing deer out of season and selling the venison to nearby lumber camps, but the evidence proved insufficient for a conviction. Hunting in the winter to supply lumber camps continued to be widespread and was the target of considerable editorial comment in *Forest and Stream* and other sporting journals.

Notwithstanding all this evidence of illegal and controversial hunting, wildlife biologists C. W. Severinghaus and C. P. Brown estimate that the Adirondack deer population probably reached a peak in 1890. By that time the lumber operations and the fires that so often followed them had penetrated nearly every part of the region (though some large individual tracts remained untouched), and practically the entire region was able to support increasing numbers of deer. Nonetheless, downstate hunters and editors continued to insist that indiscriminate shooting would eventually exterminate the Adirondack deer herd.

* * *

In 1895 the Forest Commission (which had been established in 1885) was reorganized as the Fisheries, Game and Forest Commission, one of the nation's first state-wide conservation agencies with responsibilities that included wildlife. In William F. Fox, the New York State Superintendent of Forests, the opponents of illegal hunting found a firm ally. He expressed his views on the proper way to hunt deer eloquently and cogently in the first annual report of the Commission, explicitly condemning jacking and all summer shooting. Summer hunting, he wrote, "is a mere wanton cruelty, prompted by that barbaric instinct to kill which still lingers in the human race." Pleading with the legislature to establish a rational open season, he pointed out that no other state or Canadian province allowed the killing of deer in the summer: "It was reserved for New York to frame a law based on personal interests instead of the dictates of humanity and the ethics of sport." According to Fox, if New York would prohibit jacking and all summer hunting, the deer of the Adirondacks would last forever. The bag limit, first established in 1888, had begun to eliminate market hunting.

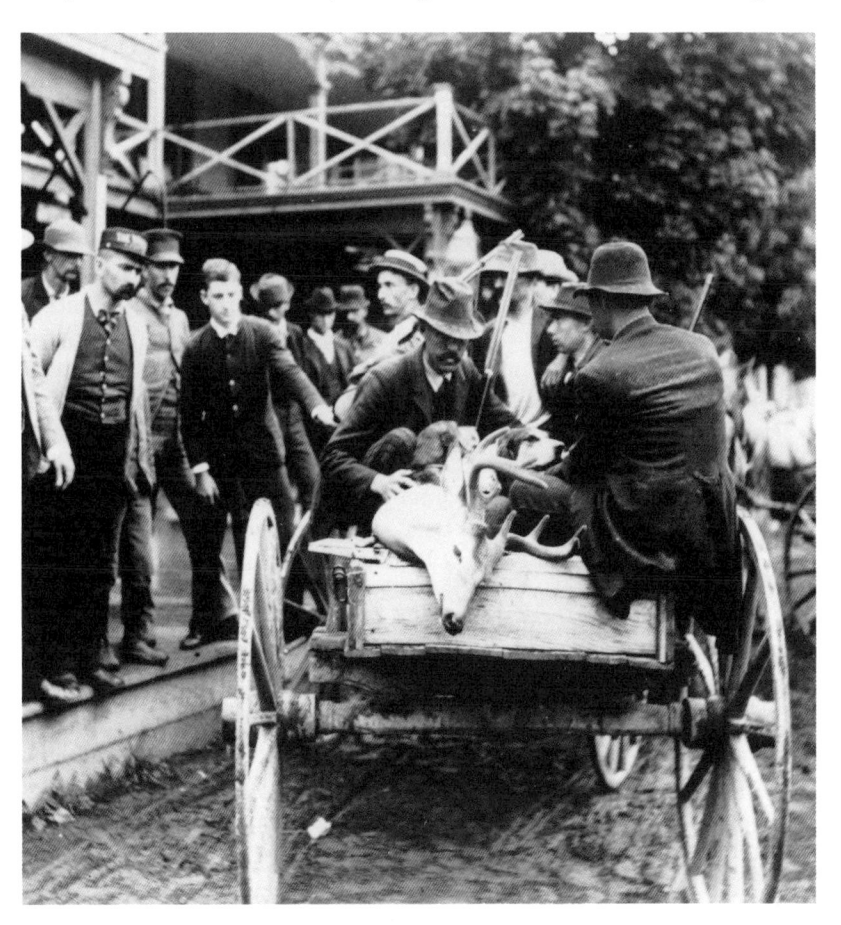

S. R. Stoddard, "At the Windsor House Hotel, Elizabethtown, 1912."
(Collection Adirondack Museum)

Finally, the legislature seemed to be listening to some of what Fox and others were saying. In 1896, restrictions were put on jacking, which was limited to the first two weeks in September, while the legal season for hounding was shortened from a month to the first two weeks in October. This part of the law failed to curtail hounding. Instead, all the hounders found themselves in the woods at the same time, and in fact 280 more deer were reported killed before the hounds in 1896 than in the longer season of the previous year. In the interests of safety Fox suggested to the lawmakers that if hounding had to be legal, the season might as well be lengthened to keep the woods less crowded. In his 1896 report Fox also urged the legislature to set the opening date of the season at October 1, again pointing out that no other state or Canadian province allowed the killing of deer before that date and that New York's law appeared to be made for "summer people," not for ethical hunters.

Fox's hope for a sensible opening date was not to be realized for some time; in 1897 the legislature again set it at August 15. But the 1897 law completely prohibited all jacking and hounding for five years after its passage. The chief agent in the passage of this law was Martin Van Buren Ives, Assemblyman from St. Lawrence County. Ives reasoned that neither jackers nor hounders would ever be happy if one group thought its sport was prohibited while the other's remained legal. In moving to prohibit jacking, the state lagged behind some of the large private preserves. The Adirondack League Club, for example, had banned jacking on its property in 1892.

In addition to the pressure coming from Ives, further opposition to hounding came from the membership of the Boone and Crockett Club, founded in 1888 to advocate conservation of the nation's natural resources. Although the Club maintained interests in wildlife issues across the country, its members, many of whom grew up in the aristocratic circles of eastern American cities, paid special attention to the Adirondacks. In 1894, one of its principal founders, Theodore Roosevelt, wrote to another prominent member, George Bird Grinnell, to suggest that the Boone and Crockett Club undertake a lobbying campaign against hounding: "Don't you think the executive committee might try this year to put a stop to hounding in the Adirondacks? Appear before the legislature, I mean. I wish to see the Club do something." The Club did lobby and considered itself partly responsible for the legislation of 1897.

In 1901 hounding was made illegal forever, and in 1902 the same step was taken for jacking. Neither of these laws was ever repealed. Game law enforcers now had a law that seemed to promise a sensible game policy, hounding having been made illegal six times from 1788 to 1901. In 1905

August hunting was prohibited, in 1909 the opening date was set at September 16, in 1912 at October 1, and in 1931 at October 26, the same year the limit was reduced to one deer.

* * *

Even with the permanent establishment of anti-hounding and anti-jacking legislation the fight was hardly over. The enforcement of the laws was nearly as difficult as ever. One man wrote to *Forest and Stream* in 1897 from Raquette Lake and observed that when the game warden was in the area, he put up in the most expensive hotel in town, and everyone knew all his comings and goings. Since most of the game protectors in the Adirondacks were local men, they were not inclined to arrest their friends and neighbors — especially when the offense was hounding — because they thought the hounding prohibition was passed to serve the interests of downstate hunters and ignored local feelings. Most guides still hoped that hounding could be legalized again, and in 1898 both the Democratic and Republican nominees for the Assembly and Senate from Essex County promised to work for the repeal of the anti-hounding law. In 1901 Assemblyman Graeff of Essex County introduced legislation to legalize hounding, but it was rejected by the Assembly. In 1912 hounding was still being practiced around Northville and presumably throughout the more inaccessible portions of the Adirondacks, but observers agreed that the law was having its effect. Hunters were gradually ceasing to use hounds because they did not want to spend the day chasing a deer only to have it confiscated upon leaving the woods.

The number of game protectors was increased to thirty-eight in 1895 and to fifty in 1902. By 1911 there were ninety for the entire state, but *Forest and Stream* insisted that there were still too few. In 1900 Lieutenant Governor Timothy Woodruff, owner of the rustic but luxurious Kamp Kill Kare near Raquette Lake, was found guilty of hunting before the opening of the deer season and fined $250. The charges against Woodruff were brought by the Brown's Tract Guides' Association at Old Forge. Undoubtedly, the local people were delighted to prosecute a downstate hunter and a politician at the same time.

Probably the most common violation of the game laws at this time was winter shooting to supply lumber camps. *Forest and Stream* editorialized in favor of legislation that would forbid the possession of any firearms in the woods during the closed season. No such bill ever became law. In 1907 *Forest and Stream* maintained again that the worst game-law offenders were the suppliers to the camps but admitted that the situation was improving with the addition of more game protectors. Logging in the Adirondacks began to decrease around that time, moreover, and because of improved roads and later the introduction of motorized transport, the logging operations that continued, except those in the most inaccessible parts of the forest, began to require fewer men to stay in camps through the winter.

Winslow Homer, "Deer Stalking in the Adirondacks in Winter" (1871).
Collection Adirondack Museum

* * *

Most of the controversy over game and game laws in the Adirondacks revolved around the white-tailed deer. But while the battle continued over the protection of deer, another struggle developed over the bear. For a century, Adirondack bears, like nearly all predators, had been persecuted unmercifully, shot at on every occasion. An 1881 incident on Lake George, reported in *Forest and Stream*, was typical. Two men traveling across the lake on a steamboat spotted a swimming bear and set out after it in a small boat armed only with an axe. After being wounded and infuriated, the bear tried to overturn the boat, but the men managed to row back to the steamboat with the bear chasing them. Once aboard the larger craft they threw a noose around the bear's neck and proceeded to drown it by putting the steamboat into full throttle and dragging the poor beast behind them.

Farmers living in the Champlain Valley maintained that they were losing valuable sheep and other stock to the predations of bears, and in 1892 the state established a ten-dollar bounty. The bounty was repealed only three years later but not before the state had paid for the heads of 907 bears; in 1894 alone 359 Adirondack bears were killed for the bounty. In 1902 *Woods and Waters*, a magazine founded and almost singlehandedly produced by Harry Radford, whose devotion to conservation in the Adirondacks earned him the sobriquet "Adirondack Harry," initiated a campaign to save the supposedly threatened Adirondack bear. In a series of passionate editorials and articles, Radford urged the legislature to protect bears with a closed season. Against stiff North Country opposition, a bill to provide a closed season passed the Senate that year. The bill set the open season at October 1 through June 1, with a limit of one bear to a hunter and a permanent prohibition on all bear traps. On the last day of the session the bill was defeated in the Assembly.

The reason for the failure of the bill was the generally held fear that bears were killing and eating domestic animals. Governor Odell himself expressed this sentiment and added his not inconsiderable support to those legislators who opposed the bill. Contrary evidence was provided to *Woods and Waters* by one R. J. Donovan, who had lived in Essex County as a boy. He asserted that bears seldom if ever killed sheep but were often accused when the culprits were actually domestic and feral dogs. (Modern wildlife specialists concede that bears do kill sheep and pigs occasionally, but dogs are thought to be responsible for much greater damage.) Donovan's view was not accepted at the time by the legislature. Although the state had discontinued its bounty on bears, Essex County did not and in 1902 paid out $280.

In a study on the Adirondack bear for the *Seventh Annual Report* of the Forest, Fish and Game Commission, George Chahoon doubted that during 1902 one sheep was killed in Essex County by a bear. The following year, the Commission declared that the bear was in danger of extirpation in New York and asked the legislature to protect it. No action was taken at the subsequent legislative session, and the Commission in its next report again requested protection for the bear. In 1903 *Woods and Waters* reported that a new bill to protect bears was before the legislature, but this bill too was headed for failure; the opposition of North Country legislators was still too strong.

The lobbying of interested sportsmen, led by Harry Radford, continued, and the bill was re-introduced in the 1904 session. On May 9, 1904,

Men weren't the only bear hunters. Stella Otis with
Adirondack black bear, circa 1912.
(Collection Adirondack Museum)

the bill was signed into law by Governor Odell. Its passage had been violently opposed, and Essex County was exempted from the new law, which provided a closed season for the months of July, August, and September. Except for that brief period, bear could still be shot at will. Not only was Essex County exempted from the provision for a closed season, but bounties were still offered in that county while the bear was protected throughout the rest of the state. In other words, the bear in Essex County was vermin while elsewhere it was a protected, therefore apparently valuable, big-game species. In Essex County in 1904, thirty-nine bounties were paid; in the rest of the state 106 bears were reported killed by sportsmen. In 1906 Essex County paid bounties on fifty-two bears, but after that year the number began to decline steadily.

A black bear dining at the Long Lake dump.
Photo by Nancie Battaglia.

In 1923 the bear was protected throughout the state. The Conservation law of that year limited the legal take to one bear a season and prohibited the use of jacklights, traps, hounds, and even airplanes in hunting bears. Since then the Adirondack black bear has expanded its range and has increasingly posed a threat to farmers, whose corn is often destroyed, and to beekeepers. In the central Adirondacks, where hunting now fails to control the bear population, hikers and camp owners often complain about bears, while the year-round residents seem to accept bears and any problems associated with them as an inevitable part of life in the North Woods. At town dumps, watching bears rummage through the garbage has become a tourist attraction.

The struggle over New York's game laws was lengthy and fierce (and included, of course, discussions of far more species than those mentioned here: during this same period extensive debate over the legal shooting of game birds — mostly ducks, grouse, and pheasants — routinely occupied the state's legislators). Moving from the laissez-faire policy of the mid-nineteenth century to the familiar seasons and limits of today, first instituted early in this century, was a difficult and contentious haul, but by 1912, the conservationist William T. Hornaday could write,

> I think we may justly regard New York as the banner state of all America in the protection of game and wild life in general. In these days of game destruction, when our country from Nome to Key West is reeking with the blood of slaughtered wild creatures, it is a privilege and a pleasure to be a citizen of a state which has thoroughly cleaned house, and done nigh well the utmost that any state can do to clear her bad record, and give all her wild creatures a fair chance to survive.

But Hornaday, an avid hunter, did not intend for animals to have "a fair chance to survive" recreational hunting. Like so many hunters of his and preceding generations, he saw the purpose of game laws to be protecting game species *for* sport hunters. To Hornaday, killing a deer for money was contemptible, while killing for sport — so long as certain codes were observed — was admirable and manly.

Hornaday's anthropocentric position on the proper attitude toward wildlife was shared by many influential Americans of the day. But a minority view was beginning to emerge. T. Madison Grant, Secretary of the New York Zoological Society, saw a special role for the Adirondacks as a new kind of preserve for wildlife. In an essay composed for the New York State Forest, Fish and Game Commission in 1905, Grant recommended a radical departure from old ways:

> Some section of the Adirondacks embracing forest, stream and lake should be set aside for a breeding ground for all the native animals, where they should be left absolutely undisturbed, and no one allowed to set a trap, light a fire or enter with a gun or dog; and above all no foreign species should be introduced. It is only a question of time when something of this sort will be done in the North Woods, and the privilege of carrying a gun at all times and slaughtering everything in sight will be abridged.

7 Extirpation and Reintroduction

WHILE THE LEGISLATURE and various deer lobbies were quarreling over protection for the white-tailed deer, the Adirondack wolf and mountain lion were dwindling down to extirpation. At the same time, the state and private clubs were attempting to restock certain species that had or were thought to have inhabited the Adirondacks—mainly beaver, moose, and elk. Of these, only the effort to restock beaver was successful; others failed because of ecological or pathological obstacles only recently understood. The species chosen for protection or reintroduction were all valued for trophies or trapping, while those eliminated, wolves and mountain lions, continued to be detested as dangerous vermin. The choices made suggest a distinct set of environmental values: the primary predator in the Adirondacks, man, remained uncomfortable with the *idea* of predation.

When C. Hart Merriam published *The Mammals of the Adirondacks* in 1884, the mountain lion and wolf, retreating under pressure from bounty hunters and increasingly limited in range by the gradual elimination of sufficiently wild habitat, were reaching the end of the line. By 1880 the killing of a mountain lion or wolf was such a rarity as to command wide attention and comment. D. H. Hurd, in his *History of Clinton and Franklin Counties*, wrote that mountain lions were still occasionally killed but that such incidents were unusual. *Forest and Stream* reported in 1880 that two mountain lions had been killed at Childwold that autumn and that the species was thought to be nearly extinct in the Adirondacks.

In 1882 outdoor writer Fred Mather traveled through the Adirondacks with Verplanck Colvin's surveying party and sent weekly columns to *Forest and Stream*. He wrote that wolves were gone from New York, and mountain lions were becoming so scarce that it might be wise to remove the bounty on them. But the notion of preserving a species in danger of disappearing

Daniel Beard, "Evicted Tenants of the Adirondacks," *Harper's Weekly* (28 Feb. 1885).

did not appeal to the majority of late-nineteenth-century Americans. Fred Mather might ponder wistfully the possibility of keeping a few mountain lions in the Adirondacks, but the average New Yorker still saw the big cat as a vicious, potentially man-eating beast.

That same year, 1882, *Forest and Stream* estimated the mountain lion population of the Adirondacks to be no more than six individuals. But only two years later the editors were beseeching the legislature to raise the bounty on mountain lions, arguing that great quantities of deer were being killed by them; complete extirpation was the solution. A couple of weeks later "R" responded to that editorial with the observation that *Forest and Stream* was raising a fuss over nothing, that there were very few mountain lions left in the Adirondacks, and that bounty money would be much more effective if it were paid for domestic dogs that were chasing deer or, on the second offense, for their owners. As before, the mountain lion was the focus of attention only to the extent that it was perceived to be preying on deer.

By 1885 most people thought both wolves and mountain lions were extirpated in the Adirondacks, and only occasional sightings and killings were reported for the rest of the century. *Harper's Weekly* ran a full-page engraving that year of the "Evicted Tenants" of the Adirondacks, declaring that the moose, elk, wolverine, beaver, mountain lion, and wolf had all been extirpated. Although most New Yorkers were indifferent to the likelihood that native species had been "evicted" from the Adirondacks, the fact that *Harper's*, a popular and influential journal, published such an illustration showed an incipient concern for preservation or restoration of the native fauna. Once a nostalgia for something lost developed, the idea of saving wild species slowly gained currency. The notion of regret was an important ingredient in the eventual effort to reintroduce at least some of the extirpated species.

A few mountain lions and wolves lingered here and there for over a decade longer (the beaver, as we shall see, was never extirpated). In 1891 rumors of wolves in the Adirondacks were rejected by state wildlife and fur expert A. N. Cheney, who maintained that only an occasional stray wandered into the region. Two years later a mountain lion, perhaps a stray from the southern Adirondacks, was killed within the city limits of Schenectady.

In 1894, according to Madison Grant, the last bounty for a mountain lion recorded killed in New York was paid in Herkimer County. Grant calculated that this was the ninety-ninth bounty paid out under the law of 1871. Although occasional sightings have been reported ever since, no clear evidence of a resident population has surfaced. In 1897 two mountain lions were believed to be in the Oswegatchie region. A couple of years later trapper David K. Mix of Long Lake said he saw mountain lion tracks in the snow south of Newcomb. That same year, 1899, *Woods and Waters*, generally more progressive on these matters than *Forest and Stream* was, argued against bounties on any species, arguing that it was unwise "to tamper with the laws of Nature or attempt to improve its even balance." This anticipates an observation by the mid-twentieth-century wildlife biologist and conservationist Aldo Leopold: "There is no such thing as a good or bad species; a species may get out of hand, but to terminate its membership in the land is the last word in anthropomorphic arrogance."

Adirondack Mountain lion as depicted in Wallace's
Descriptive Guide to the Adirondacks, 1881.

Both *Woods and Waters* and *Forest and Stream* continued to report unsubstantiated sightings of mountain lions for the next few years. In 1900 there were supposed to be one or two in both the Cold River and Bog River areas, and H. Pell Jones told John Burnham that one was seen at Elk Lake in around 1900 or 1901. "Juvenal" wrote the editors of *Forest and Stream* in 1917 in answer to an article titled "Are Panthers Coming Back?" that they had never left and that sure signs were seen in 1915. Among these were photographs of tracks in the snow near Pico Lake on Adirondack League Club property taken by Club Forester R. E. Hopson.

EXTIRPATION AND REINTRODUCTION

* * *

When George Muir, who had been killing wolves and mountain lions in St. Lawrence County for thirty years, caught a wolf in a bear trap in 1895, the editors of *Forest and Stream* uncharacteristically suggested that maybe a few wolves in the Adirondacks would not be a bad idea. But by then it was too late to save the Adirondack wolf. Persecuted by hunting and trapping, the state bounty, and by the general hatred for wolves common among

Reuben Cary poses with the remains of the last Adirondack wolf.
(Collection Adirondack Museum)

Adirondack settlers, wolves were also pressured by the gradual destruction of the wilderness by logging and fires. Nowhere in North America have wolves persisted in territory that has become relatively civilized. When the wilderness goes, so do the wolves. The state paid six bounties in each of the years 1895, 1896, and 1897, mostly in St. Lawrence and Franklin Counties. In 1899 trapper and guide Reuben Cary killed a wolf in St. Lawrence County. This was the last documented native wolf ever taken in New York. After it was stuffed and mounted, Cary posed with it for a commemorative photograph.

As with the mountain lion, rumors and purported sightings have persisted to the present. The issue of wolf sightings is complicated by the immigration to New York of coyotes in the early part of the twentieth century and the arrival of German Shepherds and other large canines which in the nineteenth century had not yet been introduced into New York. People have seen coyotes or feral dogs and sworn they saw wolves, and strays from outside the state have occasionally been taken. As late as 1984, a female wolf, presumably having wandered in from Ontario, was trapped in Allegheny County in western New York.

* * *

Efforts to restock moose in the Adirondacks began soon after the last native moose disappeared. In 1877, members of the Adirondack Club, predecessor of the Tahawus Club, procured a cow moose from Nova Scotia and had it delivered to the Upper Works. The executive report for that year records the club's wish to obtain a bull to go with its cow and the hope that the club could help to restock the entire vicinity. But as long as there were significant numbers of deer in the area, the successful introduction of moose was problematic. Of this now recognized fact, of course, the Adirondack Club and the proponents of subsequent restocking efforts had no knowledge.

The Adirondack Club entered into the project in good faith, although their motive was not completely altruistic. The members hoped some day to have on their preserve a herd of moose sufficiently large to support hunting. They also expected that some moose would inevitably escape from their preserve. They hoped that these would repopulate the vicinity, be seen as gestures of good will by the local settlers, and therefore encourage cooperation with the club's efforts to conserve the game on its own property. To protect the moose in the initial stage of this restocking project, the club saw to it that State Senator Wagstaff introduced a bill at the 1878 session of the legislature to provide a $250 fine for killing a moose at any time.

Forest and Stream endorsed this project and reported that the Adirondack Club would purchase live moose for restocking in the Adirondacks. Eventually four moose — two bulls and two cows — were secured by the Club and kept in a fenced enclosure on its grounds. Efforts to encourage them to breed and produce calves were unsuccessful, however. The 1879 report of the executive committee recorded the death, reportedly by poisoning, of two of the moose; quite possibly the moose were not poisoned at all but rather died of the brain disease. Nothing further was mentioned about this restocking effort.

EXTIRPATION AND REINTRODUCTION

In 1898 Harry Radford founded *Woods and Waters*, a short-lived but effervescent magazine devoted to hunting and hunting-related conservation. It published articles about all parts of the country but was especially concerned with the Eastern United States. In the fourth issue Radford began promoting a campaign for restocking moose in the Adirondacks. Advising his readers that as he wrote, during the winter of 1898-99, there were several private parks that had already successfully stocked moose and that within the preserve of Dr. W. Seward Webb alone there were over one hundred moose, Radford urged the Fisheries, Game and Forest Commission to obtain moose and release them throughout the Adirondacks on state land. (No other evidence suggests that so many moose were actually on the Webb property; Radford's claim appears to have been an exaggeration.) After protecting reintroduced moose for five or ten years, the state could then allow hunting in the region, which, Radford maintained, would bring to New York "twice as much attention from sportsmen."

Throughout Radford's spirited campaign, the financial benefits to the state of having moose restocked in the Adirondacks were repeatedly emphasized. Like some environmentalists of today, Radford recognized the need for persuasive arguments to win the support of an otherwise possibly indifferent readership. Radford's passionate editorials on the reintroduction of moose to the Adirondacks and what he asserted would be its benefits to the region and the state always stressed the ostensible economic advantages.

Woods and Waters began printing a series of letters from hunters and game managers throughout the Adirondacks urging the state to restore the moose. The first of these was from Charles A. Taylor, Secretary of the Fisheries, Game and Forest Commission, who promised to put the matter before the Commission at their next meeting and suggested that the only reason that it had not been considered before was a shortage of funds and the decision to use the funds that were available for restocking fish in the state's depleted rivers and lakes. In the following issue, two pages were devoted to letters from various Adirondack hunters, guides, and miscellaneous friends of the moose. One was from Verplanck Colvin, who wrote that the most important element in a successful restocking effort would be public will: "The moose and the bison and all of the rare fauna of this country could be preserved, at least in Government and State forests and reservations, if sensible, thoughtful, sympathetic people would unite to demand it." Running through nearly all these letters was the warning that any project to restore the Adirondack moose would fail unless stringent laws were passed for their protection, particularly from hunters eager for larger trophies and different sport.

WILDLIFE AND WILDERNESS

The fears of those skeptical about restocking the Adirondacks with moose were dramatically realized in 1900 when W. Seward Webb released five moose from his park. By the fall one had been shot by a Saranac Lake guide named Charles Martin who brought the meat into the village and tried to sell it. Shooting moose was illegal at that time, having been prohibited in 1878, and Martin was arrested and fined. *Forest and Stream*, never optimistic about the possibilities of a successful reintroduction of moose, com-

Moose killed near Lake Placid, 1905.
(Collection Adirondack Museum)

mented that this incident proved that the project was doomed from the start by local "lack of respect for law and decency." Even W. H. H. Murray got into the act, also fearing that any moose introduced to the Adirondacks would be shot. He, however, mistrusted the summer sportsmen more than he did the natives. *Forest and Stream* and Murray thus invoked the same arguments used in the hounding versus jacking debate. Who were the better sportsmen, local or downstate hunters?

Nonetheless, Radford zealously pursued his goal, gaining momentum and ardor with each issue. Beginning with the summer 1900 number, Radford started covering his with magazine with slogans. Running up the right-hand margin for the next few years was the motto, "The duty of N. Y.

Legislature — Restock the Adirondacks with Moose." Throughout that and subsequent issues were marginal notes, pictures, and sentimental verse reminding the reader of the struggle to restore moose to the Adirondacks. One bit of verse, by "E. N. F.," illustrates the worshipful tone Radford's campaign had assumed:

> Bring Back the Moose.
>
> Once through the North Woods,
> Stately, majestic,
> Wandered the strong moose,
> King of his kind.
> Panthers evaded him,
> Wolves turned away from him,
> Red men esteemed him
> The best of their find.
>
> Now he has passed away, —
> Only in memory
> His deep-throated bellowings
> Are borne to the ear.
> No more through upland glade,
> Splitting of wood decayed,
> Or other markings made,
> Show "a moose near."
>
> Old hunters still bemoan
> That those great lords are flown —
> Flown from the North Woods —
> Rightly their home.
> This is the cry they raise: —
> "Oh, give us back those days
> That through these forest ways
> They may yet roam."

Finally, the 1901 legislature appropriated $5000 for the purchase of moose for the Adirondacks. The bill was passed by both houses and signed into law by Governor Odell on March 21. In addition to the appropriation, the new law provided for a $500 fine for killing moose. *Woods and Waters* was ecstatic; Radford announced that negotiations were to begin at once and that within ten or twelve years New York would be the sportsman's paradise of the East.

It took the Forest, Fish and Game Commission a year to secure its first moose. On July 7, 1902, three moose (a cow and two bulls, an illogical combination) were liberated at Uncas Station, seven miles west of Raquette

Lake. By the end of the year at least fifteen moose had been liberated on state land, twelve of which were released at Uncas Station and spent the winter in two yards: just south of Raquette Lake and three miles west of Big Moose Lake. The local game protector was optimistic, but one moose was shot near Eighth Lake. In addition to the moose procured and liberated by the state about five had escaped from private preserves. *Woods and Waters* estimated that in the winter of 1902-1903 there were around twenty moose on state land and ran a dramatic drawing of a moose with the caption, "Hail to the Returning King—His Majesty the Moose!"

That winter saw the high point of the program. The following year the legislature failed to renew the appropriation for the purchase of more moose, three of the moose already released had been shot, and no calves were reported. Despite these discouraging circumstances, Madison Grant, in a paper on Adirondack Mammals for the 1903 *Report* of the Forest, Fish and Game Commission, argued for the legislature to continue its funding: "The moose can be easily restored to the Adirondacks if a sufficient number—not less than one hundred individuals—be liberated under proper precautions."

But the legislature remained intractable for two years, and when it finally did move in 1905, it appropriated only $2,149.73, or the amount left over from the original purchase fund. Even that insufficient sum was denied, however, when Governor Higgins vetoed the bill. The Forest, Fish and Game Commission, meanwhile, pleaded for more money as it saw the project lapsing into failure. Only a few of the original stock of reintroduced moose were still alive; some had been killed by hunters and some by locomotives. Finally, in the spring of 1906 the legislature offered the Commission the same $2,149.73, and the governor let it pass.

The Commission at that time was still optimistic. By 1908, however, the entire project was recognized as a failure and abandoned. The 1909 *Report* of the Forest, Fish and Game Commission announced, "Nothing has been heard from the few moose still remaining in the Adirondacks, but none were reported killed during the year." In any event, the New York debacle with moose was but one of several efforts in the eastern United States and Canada. Nearly all failed. The only exception was in Newfoundland, where transplants involving six moose between 1878 and 1904 resulted in a healthy, viable population occupying most of the island by 1945.

* * *

A bizarre and tragic consequence of the project to reintroduce moose to the Adirondacks was a privately undertaken experiment with elk. Many

"Hail to the Returning King—His Majesty the Moose!"
Woods and Waters, 4 (summer 1901).

people, including Madison Grant, who should have known better, believed that elk had at one time been common in the Adirondacks. Elk naturally inhabit prairies, prairie-like marshes, and sandy pine-and-oak stands. Of the latter there were undoubtedly a few on the Adirondack periphery, and they probably supported a few elk. But by the time the introduction attempts were made, these sandy zones were unavailable for the experiment, which was made in the central Adirondacks, a range entirely unsuited to elk.

As soon as Radford initiated his campaign for the restoration of moose, a few private preserve owners who had been stocking elk on their property both in the Adirondacks and elsewhere, decided that elk would be an equally beneficial addition to state land and offered to donate some. William C. Whitney gave twenty elk from his estate in Lenox, Massachusetts. These were shipped to the Raquette Lake Railroad station, transported across the lake on a freight boat to the Forked Lake Carry, and there liberated. Of these, sixteen were cows, and four bulls.

An anthropocentric pride resides in all these restocking attempts, in the facile belief that animals could be routinely removed from one place and successfully located in another. The enthusiasm with which both public officials and private philanthropists embraced these projects illustrates the ebullient confidence of late-nineteenth-century American attitudes toward nature. Having recently (in 1890) been told that the American frontier was closed, that American civilization had conquered the wilderness and replaced it with domestic institutions from coast to coast, Americans believed they could just as efficiently restore wilderness conditions wherever and whenever they chose.

Not unexpectedly, *Woods and Waters* greeted the notion of elk in the Adirondacks with delight and cheerfully reported further additions to the nascent Adirondack elk population. The elk survived their first Adirondack winter without much apparent difficulty, and *Woods and Waters* announced the following autumn that the herd had naturally increased to around thirty. That same fall William C. Whitney donated forty-five more elk, and with five more given by hotel owner William Dart the herd suddenly was increased to eighty. By 1903 the Forest, Fish and Game Commission, after warning the year before that the project was purely experimental, reported that 140 had thus far been liberated. Of these, four were known to have been killed by trains and eight by hunters. At the end of 1903 there were approximately 168 elk in seven Adirondack counties. A summary of the liberations to that point showed that twenty-two had been released at the Forked Lake Carry, forty at Little Tupper Lake, twenty at Raquette Lake, and seventy-three at Paul Smith's.

DON'T SHOOT!

There is no open season on

MOOSE, ELK or MEN.

Both Moose and Elk have been liberated in this vicinity, and the woods are full of Men.

The killing of a Moose or an Elk is a misdemeanor, and the penalty for such killing is

$350.00

and imprisonment for not less than three months nor more than one year.

All Sportsmen and Hunters are cautioned against shooting before knowing what they are shooting at.

Report all Violations to the

BROWN'S TRACT GUIDES' ASS'N.

Notice from Old Forge area, posted after release of moose and elk.
(Collection Adirondack Museum)

In the following *Report* (1904) the Commission declared that there were two hundred elk in the Adirondacks and that the project was a success. By 1905 the estimate was at 250, and the Commission was asking for money to purchase more in order to prevent too much inbreeding. In 1906, having obtained the necessary funds (the legislature seemed more willing to underwrite a project already begun privately and with an apparent chance of success than it was to support one yet to be proved), twenty-six more elk, five bulls and twenty-one cows, were released—seventeen at Newcomb,

"Alarmed: Elk on Little Tupper Lake, Adirondacks,"
Seventh Annual Report, New York Forest, Fish and Game Commission,
1902.

four west of Lake George Village, and five on Tongue Mountain. One of the Newcomb elk was soon shot, but the total Adirondack population at the end of 1906 was estimated to be close to 350. In 1907 the last state-financed liberation, of "a small number," took place west of Thirteenth Lake in Warren County.

As of the year of the last release, 1907, the outlook still seemed favorable, but shortly thereafter doubts began to appear. Many were shot, supposedly mistaken for deer. By 1910 the Forest, Fish and Game Commission was forced to admit that the Adirondack elk were "steadily decreasing." The reason for the decline was assumed to be the numbers shot by mistaken hunters. Through the teens the elk herd continued to decline. By 1915 the entire experiment was thought to have failed, but in that year a herd was discovered wintering west of Long Lake and there were rumors of two other herds. The newly organized Conservation Commission, because of the expected benefits of elk to the local economy in attracting tourists, hoped to protect the elk that had survived.

"An Adirondack Elk Descended from those
Liberated Fifteen Years Ago,"
New York State Conservationist, 1 (Jan. 1917).

The Benevolent and Protective Order of Elks then entered the picture and obtained a carload of perhaps twenty or twenty-five animals to be released in the Adirondacks. A few years earlier the B. P. O. E. had passed a resolution condemning the then popular practice among its membership of wearing elk teeth on watch fobs. Before that resolution had been passed (and for some time thereafter), elks had been slaughtered by the thousands all over their natural range and left to rot after their eye teeth had been extracted. Perhaps with some guilt over this destructive fad, the Elks undertook to replenish the declining Adirondack herd. The one car load seems to have assuaged that guilt, and the B. P. O. E. was not heard from again.

After 1917 there is scant further mention of elk in official publications. The first issue of the *New York State Conservationist*, the public-relations organ of the Conservation Commission, printed a photograph of a surviving Adirondack elk, and the magazine maintained that the elk were doing well. After that, the Adirondack elk quickly disappeared, although the 1942 report of the Conservation Department contains a cryptic reference to an experiment with feeding "deer cakes" to both deer and elk at the state's DeBar Mountain Game Refuge.

* * *

The solitary success in the various restocking efforts involved the beaver — mainly because the Adirondack beaver had never been completely extirpated and because suitable habitat remained available. The beaver was the only threatened or extirpated mammal whose decline was solely and directly attributable to human predation. In the cases of other animals — moose, wolf, mountain lion — the diminution of wild habitat played a major role. In 1893 the Assistant State Zoologist, William B. Marshall, declared the beaver to be extirpated in New York, but there is little question now that he was wrong. As we have seen, one or two families of native beaver had survived in the area north of Upper Saranac Lake. Harry Radford, who took up the campaign to restock beaver along with his other reintroduction projects — in this case with similar zeal and considerably greater success — estimated in 1900, before the restocking program had commenced, that in the entire Adirondacks there were no more than fifteen beaver and that they were all in one area in Township 20 north of Upper Saranac.

On the same page where Radford announced in *Woods and Waters* that the bill authorizing the restocking of moose in the Adirondacks had been signed into law, he also declared his intention to wage a similar campaign to stock elk, caribou, and beaver. The caribou project, fortunately (since caribou had not lived in the Adirondacks), was never attempted. But the beaver idea grew into a substantial effort, and by 1904 the Forest, Fish and Game Commission, with a $300 appropriation from the legislature, had acquired seven Canadian beavers from the Canadian exhibit at the Louisiana Purchase Exposition held at St. Louis that year. The animals were kept in a pen at Old Forge over the winter, and that spring, 1905, the six that were left (one of the original seven was so unpopular with the others that they killed him) were placed in the forest, two at the head of the South

Branch of the Moose River and four on the South Fork of the Main Inlet of Big Moose Lake. The Forest, Fish and Game Commission, in charge of this restocking effort as well as the others, estimated that there were forty beaver in the Adirondacks after the summer of 1905. The reason for the apparently high estimate is that in 1901 twelve had been privately released from Litchfield Park near Tupper Lake by Edward Litchfield, and in 1902 two at Lake Kora near Raquette Lake by Timothy Woodruff.

In 1906 only one beaver was released by the state, at Lake Placid, but Forest, Fish and Game commissioner Whipple was so eager to make the beaver project successful that he offered $100 out of his own pocket for the conviction of anyone who broke the 1896 law prohibiting the killing of beaver for any reason in New York. The following year the releases increased as four were liberated near Old Forge on First Lake, four on Fourth Lake, four at nearby Lake Terror, and two at Little Tupper Lake. All had come from Yellowstone National Park. In 1909 another was set free at Lake Placid, making twenty-one beavers released by the state since authorization by the legislature, in addition to fifteen released privately.

With complete protection and with these additions to the native stock, the Adirondack beaver began to thrive. It was not long before some people began to complain that the project was a bit too successful. Beaver dams and ponds were destroying valuable timber and flooding camps and roads. As the beaver population grew astonishingly rapidly in the area where they were first restocked, a number of the many private camps on the Fulton Chain were flooded in 1911. In 1912, because of the many complaints, the Conservation Commission had to remove some of the Fulton Chain beavers and replant them deeper in the wilderness. In its 1913 *Report* the Conservation Commission raised the possibility of a short open season on beaver within a few years.

By 1914 the beaver project was declared an unqualified success and the population estimated at between 1500 and 2000. The Commission observed that public sentiment generally favored having beaver in the Adirondacks although some people were opposed to any further protection because of its occasionally destructive habits. The following year the Commission had to issue permits to private individuals to destroy dams and houses where beaver had been particularly active. By 1919 the Commission was convinced that the Adirondack beaver was safely reestablished and requested the legislature to permit an open season.

Two years later a new complaint was lodged against the beaver, this time by trout fishermen, who insisted that beaver dams were ruining trout streams and prohibiting the free movement of spawning trout. The first reaction of the trout fishermen had been positive; beaver ponds had provided trout with more food and better breeding. But then the ponds grew in size, leaving tangled bushes nearly submerged where the trout could feed out of the reach of the fishermen. After the water in the ponds grew warmer, moreover, especially when more than one dam was erected on the same stream and warm water thus flowed from one pond to another, the trout began to appear scarce in certain brooks and rivers. The general opinion today is that beaver dams neither benefit nor harm trout fishing in any significant way. There are both advantages and disadvantages for trout in beaver dams and ponds. This does not mean that the subject is without controversy; many trout fishermen still detest beavers and their dams.

In 1921 the Conservation Commission estimated that there were then about 15,000 to 20,000 beaver in the Adirondacks. The following year A. B. Beakbane, a fisherman who was convinced that beaver were destroying the trout fishery in the Adirondacks, wrote confidently in *Forest and Stream* that there were at least 75,000 beaver. In the summer of that same year, *Fur News and Outdoor World*, responding to the attacks made by fishermen, asserted that there were no more than 3000 beaver in the Adirondacks. Whatever the case, in 1923 the legislature authorized the Commission to open the season on beaver as it saw fit. Not only did this law confirm the successful reintroduction and reestablishment of the Adirondack beaver, but it also set a precedent in that the law did not itself set the dates for the open season. For the first time, the legislature recognized the authority of professional biologists to determine open and closed seasons.

For years New York game regulations had been susceptible to the self-serving arguments of hunters, trappers, and others and had been set in the politically volatile arena of the legislature. As we have seen, the history of the New York game laws is a tortuous patchwork of contradictory statutes dictated by factional bias and a consistent disregard for what would be most likely to guarantee a stable population. But with the 1923 beaver law, the law makers removed the establishment of open seasons, at least for beaver, from politics. The Conservation Commission and its successor agencies would not be free from pressure from special-interest groups, but they would be employing current scientific knowledge rather than political necessity to manage the game species of New York. Except for the white-tailed deer, seasons and bag limits for all species are now set by the Department of Environmental Conservation.

In 1924 the Commission declared an open season on beaver in Clinton, Essex, Franklin, Hamilton, Herkimer, Oneida, St. Lawrence, Saratoga, and Warren counties, and certain towns in Lewis County. So many beaver were taken during this first open season that complaints subsided, and the season remained closed until 1928, when beaver could be taken during the month of March. In those days a good beaver pelt was worth about forty dollars; 5000 were taken that year in Adirondack counties.

* * *

These three species — moose, elk, and beaver — were the main focus of the reintroduction schemes of the late nineteenth and early twentieth centuries. There were plans for introduction of other species not native to the Adirondacks in historic times, but these were never pursued. Verplanck Colvin, among others, was convinced that caribou had once inhabited the Adirondacks and named a well known pass for it. In an 1890 speech to a farmers' organization, the always eccentric Colvin argued for introducing, in addition to moose and caribou, mountain goats and big horn sheep. *Woods and Waters* also suggested the possibility of introducing caribou to the Adirondacks, but the scheme never gained much of a following. Madison Grant specifically argued against it.

Equally odd was the suggestion made in 1892 by Forest Commissioner Cox that wild boar be released in the Adirondacks. The state never became involved in stocking wild boar, but a few years later Edward Litchfield imported several from Germany and released them on his estate west of Long Lake. They all apparently escaped. Some died during the winter, and a few were reported shot the following year. Apparently nothing was heard from them again. In 1972 about seven wild boars were discovered in the Indian Lake area. Two shoats were killed by automobiles on the road between Indian Lake and Sabael. That these were descended from the ones released by Litchfield around the turn of the century seems unlikely. Most bizarre of all was the plan, introduced as a bill in the 1907 legislature by Assemblyman Hooper of Essex County, to purchase a small herd of bison to be established in Essex, Hamilton, and Warren counties. The figure Mr. Hooper set as the necessary appropriation, $20,000, probably explains why the bill did not pass. Although woodland bison may well have inhabited areas on the Adirondack periphery and may have been hunted by Indians there, the central Adirondacks would have been entirely unsuitable for this species.

8   The Wildlife Bureaucracy

DURING THE LATE NINETEENTH CENTURY, New Yorkers began to worry about the future of the Adirondacks. While hunters and other campers had been enjoying recreation, lumberjacks had been cutting trees, driving logs down rivers, and seriously altering the character of the forest. Slowly, people noticed what was happening. They were particularly concerned about the effects of uncontrolled logging on the capacity of Adirondack slopes to hold water. If all the trees were cut, they feared, what had been the gradual release of the accumulated runoff of snow and rain into the state's rivers would become an endlessly repeated cycle of flood and drought. Although railroads were carrying an increasingly greater share of the state's commerce, canal and river trade remained substantial. Thus the role of Adirondack forests in maintaining adequate water for the Erie Canal, Hudson River, and other transportation arteries seemed overwhelmingly critical to the state's economy.

The story of the steps leading to the creation of the Adirondack Forest Preserve in 1885, the Adirondack Park in 1892, and the constitutional protection of the Forest Preserve in 1895 appears in many local histories. It is a dramatic episode in the evolution of the ways Americans have dealt with the natural environment. Usually we think of these events in terms of the protections afforded the forests of the Adirondacks, but there were important implications for wildlife as well. The key element is the clause of the 1895 New York State Constitution prohibiting all logging on state land: "The lands of the state, now owned or hereafter acquired, constituting the forest preserve, as now fixed by law, shall be forever kept as wild forest lands. They shall not be leased, sold, or exchanged, nor shall the timber thereon be sold, removed or destroyed." The original intent of this clause was to save the forests and thus protect the Adirondack and Catskill watersheds. But in terms of wildlife, it also stopped, at least on state land, the processes that promoted an expanding deer population. As the lands owned by the state lost their edge conditions and as the state acquired more land, the availability of browse for deer diminished. At the same time, the eventual restoration of an environment suitable for wilderness species like moose, wolves, and mountain lions became a possibility.

These changes occurred slowly, even imperceptibly. Much of the land in the public domain at the turn of the century had been recently logged, burned, or both. Much of the land subsequently bought or otherwise acquired by the state for the Forest Preserve was in a similar condition. For a while, state land provided excellent deer range, and the hunting was good. But, inexorably, the forests in the public domain matured, the canopy closed, and the deer population dwindled. It by no means disappeared, but it shrank. Some hunters argued that the truly big, trophy bucks continued to show up on state land, where the increasingly wild conditions provided a hunting experience unavailable on the more managed private preserves, but eventually it became common wisdom throughout the Adirondacks that the longer a piece of property had been in the Forest Preserve, the fewer deer it was likely to support.

* * *

In the twentieth century the Forest Preserve has grown into forty percent of the land inside the Blue Line, the Adirondack Park itself has been enlarged several times, and legislated controls have taken gradual effect over such activities as hunting and trapping. After the game laws were set, New Yorkers looked in new directions for a way to keep and increase the deer herd. The new science of game management, which developed as a distinct branch of biology in the 1920s, was the obvious vehicle for maintaining and broadening the economic base supplied by Adirondack hunting.

The history of game management in New York for the first sixty or seventy years after conservation measures were adopted in the 1880s and '90s consistently indicated that the Conservation Commission and its successor agencies existed in large measure to produce white-tailed deer. Deer became the cattle of the Adirondacks. To this day, some wildlife biologists, aware of the political significance of the Adirondack deer and frustrated by public attitudes, refer to it as the "golden calf." Yet the problem continues to be that the Adirondacks simply do not provide ideal range for producing large numbers of healthy deer. The constitutional restrictions on cutting timber in the Forest Preserve prohibit the only efficient method to sustain deer during severe winters when the snows are so deep that deer cannot secure sufficient food. The combination of Adirondack climate and Article Fourteen (the forever-wild provision as re-approved in the state constitution of 1938) substantially precludes effective deer management on state land.

This ineluctable fact, however, was not immediately recognized. In 1906 the Chief Game Protector, John Burnham, believed that the only hope for deer in the Adirondacks lay in the rapid and complete acquisition of all lands in the Park by the state. At that time lumbering operations on private land, although they were providing abundant supplies of food on cut-over acreage, were also destroying the cover that deer need to protect them from the harsh winds and cold of an Adirondack winter. Burnham assessed the condition of yarding areas on private land and concluded that the deer were yarding only on state land. The flaw in his argument that the State should therefore acquire more land for the sake of the wintering deer stemmed from the condition of the forest on state land, which was largely young growth, having been recently lumbered or burned. As that forest matured, browse would diminish; state land would become less useful for maintaining deer through severe winters.

Some hunters soon insisted, moreover, that the state should lend a hand and help the deer make it through the winter on state land. *Forest and Stream* editorialized in 1907 in favor of cutting browse for deer and making clearings near shelter during periods of deep snow and severe cold. For most of this century there have been periodic attempts either to circumvent or to amend the constitution to permit the state to cut browse for deer during winters of deep snows. They have been advanced with virtually one thought in mind—the economic benefits to the Adirondacks that a large deer herd can provide. The Adirondack economy, seldom robust, depends in the fall on hunters. Many local merchants make it from one year to the next with the money they make during hunting season. Thus far the constitution has withstood schemes to permit cutting browse for deer on state land, although feeding deer in the winter remains a widespread practice on private preserves.

In 1911 a new Conservation Law established the Conservation Commission, one of whose first actions was to undertake a program of cutting hay on beaver meadows, salting it, and stacking it on racks in the winter deer yards. This practice continued for several years, and the Commission claimed positive results: "the supply of deer in the Adirondacks is greater than at any time during the past quarter of a century." Recent research has shown, however, that hay does not satisfy the nutritional requirements of the white-tailed deer. When deer began to starve again, the program was abandoned. Probably other circumstances, such as mild winters or unusual success for Adirondack hunters convinced the Commission at the time that the program was working. Around the middle of the century the Conservation Department began cutting white cedar boughs—one of the white-tailed deer's favorite and most beneficial winter foods—into forty-pound bales and dropping them from airplanes into deer yards where deer were experiencing extreme difficulty in securing food. Such measures were seen as emergency responses only.

* * *

Meanwhile, illegal hunting was enjoying a renaissance (if, in fact, it had ever declined). In 1906, the Forest, Fish and Game Commission reported that hounding, summer shooting, and killing deer for lumber camps were all decreasing, but by 1918 the Conservation Commission began receiving "apparently authentic reports of wholesale violations of the deer laws in the Adirondacks." Game protectors were sent out on secret missions. They discovered "general contempt for the Conservation Law." Infractions included shooting does and fawns, use of dogs, and violation of bag limits (in 1918 the bag limit was two, does could not be shot after October 31, and fawns could never be killed). The findings of the game protectors, wrote the Commissioners in their annual report for that year, were "nothing short of astounding. No good will come from blinking at the facts. Practically every possible violation of the deer law was encountered by the protectors, and not once, but repeatedly." The Commissioners asserted further that no single class of hunters was more at fault than any other. For years various classes of hunters had been blaming others for breaking the law, but the Conservation Commissioners, observed that "Men of all walks of life are involved." They added that women, too, were hunting illegally.

Local newspapers complained about the underhanded methods employed by the Conservation Commission to get arrests and convictions, but the Commissioners asserted that in no other way could they both enforce the laws and convince the average Adirondack hunter that they meant business. The problem persisted, however: in 1921 the Commissioners reported "numerous complaints of the wholesale slaughter of deer and total disregard for the laws giving protection to the wild life of the State in the Adirondack Mountains." (The reports usually use the two-word term, "wild life.")

In 1927, 6,344 persons were prosecuted throughout the state for violation of the game laws, and the Conservation Department (as it was then called) commented in its annual report to the legislature, "It would appear as though there is no limit to the number of persons it is possible in the course of a year to apprehend violating the conservation laws of the state." By 1926 the number of game protectors state-wide had been increased to 150. The following year, for the first time, every deer hunter in the state was required to purchase a special license at the cost of $1.25 to residents and $10.50 to others. That year 72,841 licenses were sold in New York State.

The raw numbers of violators of game statues does not necessarily indicate any sudden public inclination to defy the law. Hunters were undoubtedly hunting as they always had. The new feature in the picture was the bureaucratic apparatus designed to sell licenses, count deer, apprehend law breakers, and generally supervise what in the nineteenth century had been an utterly uncontrolled activity. After the 1920s, the Conservation Commission annual reports show diminishing attention to game law violations, probably because the enforcement features of the law were working and because a certain level of illegal hunting is inevitable, undetectable, and impossible to prevent. Game wardens, moreover, who usually live in the area where they are enforcing the laws, are doubtless willing to wink at certain violations, especially if the transgressor is a local man getting meat for his family.

* * *

In the twentieth century, game management has emerged as one of the many focuses of a huge conservation bureaucracy. Wildlife biologists, game wardens, and other public officials, trained in colleges and graduate schools, have tried to impose order on what had formerly seemed chaos. They reflect our culture's reliance on the services of experts in dealing with complicated affairs, especially in matters of science and nature. In New York State, particularly in the Adirondacks, the focus of this bureaucracy has been the white-tailed deer. Although the 1911 Conservation Law noted that one of the chief functions of the new Conservation Commission was the "protection and propagation of fish and game," it was deer that consistently received the most attention.

The emergence of wildlife management as a legitimate activity of the state was partly a function of the difference between European and American concepts of wildlife ownership. In Europe, where wildlife had traditionally belonged to whoever held title to the land on which it was found, the responsibility for regulating populations and otherwise caring for the wildlife fell to the owners, who often hired gamekeepers or, later, foresters with wildlife training. But in North American law, animals belong to the people of the state or province; hence the responsibility for monitoring their health or for keeping populations stable likewise devolves upon public authorities. And by the third decade of this century, officials in New York and throughout the continent began to see wildlife as a renewable resource to be managed in perpetuity for the good of the people. The problem has been determining precisely what "the good of the people" means. A more recent perplexity has arisen when some people have insisted that managers should examine more than utilitarian or economic issues.

Although the state had earlier passed legislation concerning open seasons and hunting methods, this merely reflected the commonly held view that wildlife populations were in a perpetual state of decline and that measures to postpone their disappearance were needed. In this century, however, the state moved beyond this mainly police function and committed itself to producing, protecting, and managing its wildlife resources. Whereas in the past it had tried to control how and how many animals were killed, now it saw itself as the actual producer of the animals. The reasons for this concern were often vaguely articulated. The 1918 report of the Conservation Commission, in a section titled "Importance of Increasing Wildlife," noted the "value of hunting and fishing and out-of-door sport in the development of the highest type of American manhood and womanhood." Wildlife, the report continued, is "necessary for the well-being and happiness of the people of New York State in so many different ways, economic, physical and aesthetic."

As a consequence of this concern, however vague its rationale, the state soon established a scientific branch of the conservation bureaucracy, whose sole purpose was to investigate the populations and health of game species. Beginning in 1919, the annual reports listed "Biological Investigations." While earlier the Commission had been conducting censuses, it now undertook to "show the important place which wild life holds in the economy of the state." Making no effort to conceal the true impetus behind this interest in science, the 1919 Report declared that the subject of investigation was "economic biology," and the goal "the fullest possible use of the State's wild life resources." Also in 1919 the Commission requested the legislature to designate funds for paying a professional biologist or naturalist "to devote his entire time to the study of the wild life over which the Commission has jurisdiction, and regarding which it must constantly have the most dependable information." Although the reports speak endlessly of "wild life," the actual work of the naturalists hired shows that the only wildlife that really mattered was the white-tailed deer.

The thrust of the scientific investigations of the Conservation Commission consistently appeared as part of an effort to keep the state's hunters supplied with deer. In 1920 the Commission argued for additional research money to insure that "the supply of game can be continuously maintained under the democratic conditions of open hunting that have always characterized American sport." This statement reflects the Commission's awareness of the history of class-based antagonisms among different groups of hunters. If deer can be produced in sufficient numbers, the argument implies, there will be enough for everyone, rich or poor. As hunting pressure increased from all quarters, moreover, the state faced the "immediate necessity of learning the facts about our wild life resources, of eliminating guess work, and of administering our remaining stock upon a more rational and scientifically efficient basis." What in the often sentimental, anthropomorphizing nineteenth century had been a "noble buck" is thus by the 1920s but one of the state's "wild life resources."

As historian Samuel Hays has demonstrated well, one of the chief characteristics of the Progressive response to nature was to reduce it to a resource to be managed by experts. That is precisely what was happening to the wild animals of New York State (of which a substantial portion survived only in the Adirondacks), where wildlife was to be "administered" according to the precepts of rationality, science, and efficiency. Comparing the needs of wildlife management to another natural resource also moving into the domain of academically trained experts, the Commissioners maintained that the greatest advance possible in "conservation of wild life resources will be the application to this task of such scientific and exact methods of analysis and practice as have come to characterize the science of forestry." The reports of the Conservation Commission throughout the 1920s repeatedly dwell on the importance of wildlife to the state's economy. This economic factor (which was undoubtedly significant) is then invoked in appeals for more game wardens and more money for research. What emerges is a picture of a growing bureaucracy justifying its own growth, using statistics and tables to prove the need for even more management of the state's wildlife.

The vocabulary of game management became a double-barreled affair. On the one hand, we find the scientific jargon of academia—discussions, for example, of natality, pathology, and mortality; and we see agents of the state's conservation bureaucracy publishing articles in academic journals, as they strive to establish the scholarly legitimacy of their work. On the other hand, the basic reason behind this interest in biology remains purely economic. In 1932, when a new Bureau of Game was established, the Commissioners candidly admitted, "In the strictest sense the management of these resources is a business, calling for much the same methods as would be employed in operating poultry plants or cattle ranches. The object is to produce economically the largest possible amount of the most desirable resources." Two years later an equally interesting definition of the value of game appeared in a Conservation Commission Report: "Game represents an annual crop composed of capital (brood stock) and surplus and as such is capable of satisfying increase under proper management." And always behind such references to "resources" was the barely covert understanding that the only resource most people were interested in was the deer. It was the deer that were counted—alive and dead—and it was the deer whose habits were the chief, almost the exclusive, focus of research.

This obsession with deer led inevitably to dissatisfaction with the constitution. State foresters had never been content with the forever-wild provision prohibiting forestry in the Forest Preserve. And by the 1930s wildlife specialists were equally opposed to continuing this restriction. In 1935, as the state was preparing for a constitutional convention, game managers persuasively lobbied the New York State Planning Board to recommend changes in the forever-wild policy. The Planning Board advocated an amendment to the constitution allowing "the cutting of timber to provide food for deer." When a new constitution was approved in 1938, it did indeed specify that wildlife conservation was the official policy of the state, but it did not permit timber cutting as a form of wildlife management.

* * *

Shortly before World War I, the first newcomer to Adirondack wildlife in modern history arrived. The coyote, thought to have been embarked on a gradual eastern migration from the western United States, probably entered New York from Ontario at about that time. A minority theory holds that the eastern canid known as the coyote had inhabited the forests of New York before that and had been misidentified as a wolf; according to this theory, it was only after the true wolf had been extirpated that the smaller canid was distinguished. In any case, the eastern (and western) coyote has been hated, hunted, trapped, and mythologized.

The eastern coyote is a dog-like animal usually weighing under forty pounds, whose color ranges from reddish brown through various shades of gray. Coyotes are often mistaken for wolves and are commonly assumed to be much larger than they really are. And the Adirondack coyote may indeed be a more lupine creature than its western cousin. If, as seems most likely, the ancestors of our Adirondack coyote migrated north of the Great Lakes, passing through parts of Ontario where a native wolf population had survived, they may have interbred with wolves and thus acquired a proportion of wolf genes. Research involving comparative measurements of wolf and both western and eastern coyote skulls appears to confirm this hypothesis. If true, it would explain why the coyotes of New York and other eastern states are larger than western coyotes.

Ever since the coyote first appeared in the Adirondacks it has been accused of serious predations on livestock and deer, and it is true that coyotes can and do kill some deer and stock animals. In some measure, coyotes filled the predator's niche left empty by the extirpation of the wolf and mountain lion. In the winter, deer meat constitutes the major source of food for coyotes. Largely because of its predatory habits, the coyote has been persecuted with a fervor matched only by the fury which earlier killed off the wolf and mountain lion. The coyote, however, has been able to survive and even thrive in relative proximity to its most dangerous enemy and has persisted in the Adirondacks and throughout similar wild and semi-wild regions in the United States.

The campaign against the coyote in the Adirondacks has been fearsome. No evidence suggests that coyotes contribute to a decline in the deer herd. In fact their presence may be a benefit to deer by culling out sick and senile deer who would otherwise consume good browse. Some biologists maintain that the appearance of deer (or even livestock) signs in coyote stomachs or scats merely represents coyote utilization of carrion. Nonetheless, there have been bounties and trapping programs aimed at coyotes throughout the Adirondacks. More than once the Conservation Department has explicitly stated that coyotes in the Adirondacks were doing no one any harm but later yielded to local pressure and commenced intensive trapping. The December-January, 1950-51, issue of the *Conservationist*, for instance, declared that coyotes could never be a threat to the deer herd in the Adirondacks and that if the animal had any effect at all, it would be beneficial. But just six months later in the same magazine the Department announced plans for a trapping program that summer. Deer hunters and residents of the Adirondacks were (and many remain) convinced that any animal that preyed on deer could not be anything but deleterious. Evidence to the contrary supplied by downstate conservationists and Department officials was routinely ignored. The white-tailed deer remained, in many minds, the most important product of the North Country, and coyotes were perceived as a threat to the local economy.

By 1949 seven counties—Franklin, Hamilton, Jefferson, Lewis, St. Lawrence, Warren, and Washington—were paying bounties on coyotes. In the winter of 1949-50 sixty-one coyotes were killed for bounties in those counties, thirty-nine in St. Lawrence County. Although the Conservation Department had publicly observed that bounties had no real effect on coyote numbers, the state did nothing to counteract these county statutes, to convince Adirondack residents and deer hunters that coyotes offered no substantial threat to the deer population, or to demonstrate that even if they did the bounty system would not help. The bounty is a political lever, used by legislators and public officials to prove their concern and at the same time spread a little state money around their constituency. As wildlife biologist C. H. D. Clarke commented in his 1972 report to the Temporary Study Commission on the Future of the Adirondacks, "Basically, predator control survives as a sop to public prejudice." Bounties of any sort are now illegal in New York.

Meanwhile, state agents were active in trapping and otherwise trying to control coyotes. The first mention of the coyote in a Conservation Department report appears in 1949, where an investigation of a coyote-dog hybrid is described. The following year the Adirondack Game Management District reported destroying coyote dens. For the next decade the same district documented its efforts — generally by trapping — to minimize the Adirondack coyote population.

In 1991 the Department of Environmental Conservation estimated the coyote population of northern New York at 18,000 animals, with about 2,000 in Hamilton County alone. They concentrate around lowland swamps and near settlements, where deer and hare, their primary prey species, are most common. And the coyote continues to be trapped and shot — at the current rate of about 200-300 per year in the Adirondacks. But now the state has declared the coyote to be a protected species. In order to protect the state's valuable fisher population, which appeared to suffer from indiscriminate coyote trapping, the state controls coyote trapping, with an open season running from late October through March. Trappers have been able periodically to sell coyote pelts, although recently the market has been weak. Out of season, the coyote is protected, but farmers whose livestock appears threatened by coyotes may trap or shoot them at any time and without a license. And deer hunters continue to see the coyote as their chief competitor, responsible for serious depredations on the Adirondack deer herd, despite several studies showing that coyotes have no serious impact on population levels.

Coyote expert Marc Bekoff has written, "More is known about the ecology of coyotes than perhaps any other carnivore. Much of the information has been collected because of control and management interests." On occasion the coyote has been labeled a "dispensable species." Following the dictates of its inherited urge to survive and reproduce, the coyote skillfully preys on those species it can hunt with success. Sometimes these are species — such as big game animals or livestock — valued by humans. As a consequence, it becomes hated and persecuted, even though, as Bekoff remarks, "coyote control has been relatively ineffective." One of the remarkable features in the coyote story is the prodigious extent of human attempts to eradicate it combined with the amazing capacity of the coyote to survive, adapt, and even increase. Admiration for the coyote's ability to withstand persecution has become part of American folklore, appearing, for example, in a 1991 *New York Times* editorial commenting on "New York's Clever Coyotes": "Thus does the coyote thrive even after centuries of determined human assault. Rather than mindlessly continuing that campaign, humans look better admitting defeat, and granting coyotes the right to a survival they have earned."

The coyote has not been the only target of twentieth-century eradication campaigns. Starting in 1919, the Conservation Commission began requesting on every hunting license that all hunters help "destroy the enemies of useful wildlife." Among the mammals deemed "hostile to the continuance of our useful species," were the lynx, red and gray foxes, weasel, porcupine, bobcat, otter, fisher, and red squirrel. In 1921 the Commissioners reported that the response of hunters was "very gratifying." For several years the Commission included this request on hunting licenses and dutifully reported to the legislature each year that the animals "whose influence investigation proved is more harmful than good" were being eliminated by conscientious hunters. By the 1930s the state had concluded that absolute elimination of these species would not be an overall gain, aiming instead, while actively promoting game species, "to hold in check those not so desirable and which are generally classed as predators. [These] are picturesque and interesting and should never be exterminated." Fortunately, these species were not eliminated, most likely because such a haphazard program is ineffective.

Although many deer hunters continue to identify the coyote as a major competitor, one that the state ought to eliminate, attitudes toward this and other predators have undergone important changes since the coyote first appeared in the Adirondacks. First seen as a varmint, a bad animal, to be killed off through bounties, the coyote was the target of trapping, den destruction, poison, and other forms of persecution. But with the gradual penetration of ecological thinking into the public consciousness, many people have come to accept all predators as legitimate members of the Adirondack wildlife community. This line of thinking rejects the old distinction between good species and bad ones. Campers in the Adirondack backcountry treasure the memory of hearing coyotes barking at night. Those who want to see predators killed off no longer have the only voice. Many Americans, including many people interested in the Adirondacks, accept the idea of nature as a complex, interactive community where animals that eat other animals are essential to the ecosystem, possessing inherent value. In this view, the chief goal of conservation is protecting all of nature as an interdependent system.

* * *

While the deer was the most important economically and thus the most investigated of the Adirondack mammals, interest in the smaller fur bearers continued into the twentieth century. The beaver, as we have seen, grew in numbers between the turn of the century and the twenties from nearly none to a population able to withstand periodic trapping. Except for the beaver, though, none of the other valuable fur bearers in the state was given legal protection until later in the century. Among the animals trapped in New York and sold for a profit in 1918 were skunk, mink, raccoon, red and gray foxes, ermine, muskrat, bear, fisher, otter, and marten. Certain of these species, such as the otter and fisher, apparently presented the game manager with the dilemma of possessing some value on the fur market but not enough to cancel out their purported predations on other more valuable species. So whereas they were being trapped for a profit in 1918, they were vermin by 1921 and their persecution was encouraged by the Conservation Commission.

Both species received eventual protection, the fisher being first protected in 1937 and the otter at around the same time. The fisher was completely protected for thirteen years until 1949 when a short trapping season was opened. At that time the Adirondack fisher was practically the only representative of its species left in the East. The Conservation Department estimated that the supply of fisher and marten was greater in Hamilton County alone than in any other place east of the Rockies. In 1949, 113 fishers were trapped in Adirondack counties. The otter population in the Adirondacks was not high: in 1950 only thirty-six were trapped in Adirondack counties. A year later 121 were trapped with three-fifths being taken in Hamilton, Franklin, and St. Lawrence counties. The population grew slowly, however, and in 1964-65, 282 otter pelts were taken from Adirondack counties. Twenty years later, during the 1985-86 trapping season 361 otter pelts were reported in the districts that included the Adirondacks. This figure also covers some areas outside the Blue Line, so it is hard to say exactly how trapping success rates have changed.

The phenomenally successful return of the beaver to the Adirondacks allowed periodic open seasons through the 1930s and '40s as the population grew past the capacity of particular ranges to support it and as Adirondack residents and camp owners lost the patience to deal with flooded land and roads. By the early 1950s the beaver had so established itself in the Adirondacks that open seasons were held every year, and for a few enterprising Adirondack natives the beaver pelt trade became profitable indeed. In 1951, 4365 pelts were taken in Adirondack counties. During the 1985-86 season North Country trappers reported taking 5460 beaver pelts (as with the otter, this last figure includes pelts taken outside the Blue Line).

* * *

But throughout the present century the chief focus of interest, management, and controversy has continued to be the white-tailed deer. In the annual reports submitted to the legislature by the Conservation Commission and its successors, we encounter page after page describing the efforts of the conservation bureaucracy to count, survey, enlarge, and improve the Adirondack deer herd. The program wherein marsh hay was cut and salted early in the century was but the first of many similar schemes. In the 1930s game managers experimented with cakes of concentrated food and with bales of alfalfa fed to deer in winter yards in the Moose River Plains.

For the most part, however, given the exigencies of the constitution, the state could do little more than watch the deer herd, monitor its suffering in harsh winters, and report whatever evidence it could gather—at first, mostly anecdotal—on the growth or decrease of the Adirondack deer population. For example, we find "deer increasing" in 1913 and 1914. In 1919 and 1923, however, the deer herd was reported to be declining. Throughout this century, as census procedures have become more sophisticated, a similar pattern appears. In one year the deer herd is said to be healthy and growing, while only a year later the opposite is reported. All this merely illustrates the difficulty the conservation bureaucracy faced in trying to manage a game species existing on a huge range only marginally able to support it and further limited by the state constitution.

The one management mechanism available to the state, however, was control of open season, bag limits, and the determination of what age or sex could be taken. In 1912 the state tried a new "buck law," whereby hunters were prohibited from taking deer unless they had antlers at least three inches long. Many hunters objected to this restriction on what they considered their traditional freedom. During the 1919 season, the state permitted the shooting of does for the first time in several years. This resulted in controversy as well, as game managers insisted that too many were taken, with a negative effect on the total population. In 1926, in its annual discussion of the Adirondack deer situation, the Conservation Commission admitted the political difficulties involved in trying to protect "the deer herd, one of the state's most valuable possessions." Every hunter, declared the

Commissioners, is an expert and wants to promote his own version of the most efficient controls on length of season, sex or age of deer, and bag limit. The following year, the Commissioners lamented the endless "propaganda that reaches the Department on the deer question."

White-tailed deer. Photo by Nancie Battaglia.

The situation has not changed. In trying to manipulate the deer season, the state finds itself inevitably subject to second guessing from the public. The shooting of does in the Adirondacks has long been a topic of much debate. Professional game managers have maintained for some time that the Adirondack herd would be better off if a certain number of does were shot each year. Many hunters have rejoined with the obvious argument that a dead doe cannot produce fawns and that therefore the more does left alive the more offspring they will supply for future hunters. In an area like the Adirondacks, however, where winter browse is the crucial factor in the survival of a deer, scientists have found that a large number of poorly fed deer fair much worse and produce fewer healthy offspring than do smaller numbers who are securing adequate nutrition in the winter. But the doe seasons have been nearly universally condemned.

In considering the possibility of a doe season or other variations in the deer laws, moreover, the conservation bureaucracy has been further hamstrung by the refusal of the legislature to surrender jurisdiction over these laws. The legislature has empowered the state's conservation agencies to use both its own research and that of other scientists, to set open seasons and otherwise to manage the harvest of every game species in New York *except* the white-tailed deer. Beaver, bear, fisher, and coyote — for these and every other trophy or fur-bearing animal the state's own trained experts determine the season, the bag limit, and the all the variables of hunting and trapping. For the deer, however, the "golden calf," the legislature retains authority. No other feature of this story so dramatically illustrates the deer's political and economic significance.

9 "The Hallmark of Quality"

WILDERNESS IS MORE than uncut trees. It is also wildlife habitat, and a forest without its indigenous wildlife does not deserve to be called wilderness. Often we think of wilderness as the place where certain activities are not allowed—snowmobiling, for example—or where certain structures are not permitted, such as ranger stations or fire lookout towers. In this sense, wilderness appears to be defined negatively, as the opposite of more settled or managed areas. A different, more positive way to think about wilderness is in terms of wildlife populations. Do indigenous species live there, including, or even especially, the big predators? Have certain species become over-represented? What can be done to restore original populations? The extent to which a wildlife community manifests human interference in the environment measures the extent to which it fails to satisfy wilderness criteria. Can an Adirondack Forest Preserve without eastern timber wolves legitimately be called wilderness? Without mountain lions? Without a viable, reproducing moose population? Above all, will state policies aim to promote deer for hunters, or will they move toward restoration of the wildlife community of two centuries ago?

Current hopes for restoration of the indigenous Adirondack species are a far cry from the deer-dominated policies of only a few decades ago. Into the 1950s, the state conservation agencies were lobbying for the right to employ what it called "habitat management" on Forest Preserve land. This would mean cutting a certain amount of state-owned timber to open the canopy and provide new growth and browse for deer in the winter. At the time (and currently) such a practice was (and is) illegal and therefore unavailable as a management technique. Emergency measures like dropping bales of white cedar from airplanes into winter yards are prohibitively expensive and have been seldom employed. More recently, the Department of Environmental Conservation has tempered its enthusiasm for habitat management, though many deer hunters have not.

One of the most telling episodes in the history of the state's efforts to decide how best to manage the Forest Preserve occurred in the early 1950s. In the December-January, 1951–52, issue of the *Conservationist*, shortly after the great windstorm of November, 1950, known as the "Big Blowdown," the Conservation Department published a series of articles on the necessity and definition of the Forest Preserve; these precipitated a controversy soon known as the "Big Blowup of 1951." In the series the department dealt with four main questions, one of which was the place and future of wildlife on Forest Preserve land in the Adirondacks. "What is meant by 'forever wild,'" asked the editor of the *Conservationist*. "Does it suggest an abundance of birds and animals and if so, does our present management policy promote that objective?"

Answering its own question, the *Conservationist* declared, more or less accurately, that forests kept "forever wild" are not the most conducive to large populations of certain species (meaning deer) and argued that the constitutional restrictions should be loosened or even removed. In subsequent issues, officials of the Conservation Department pursued this argument against the constitution and its forever-wild provision. Two game managers, admitting that the original Adirondack forest had not been a "great wildlife reservoir," nonetheless insisted that in order for them to do their jobs the restrictions of forever wild ought to be lifted. One result of this attack on the constitution was the establishment of a Joint Legislative Committee on Natural Resources, before which Conservation Department spokesmen continued to invoke the wildlife argument to lobby against forever wild. Citing a United States Forest Service study, one official openly called for logging the Forest Preserve, maintaining that a desirable consequence would be improved wildlife habitat. While logging may in fact be good for deer, it is obviously incompatible with any reasonable definition of wilderness.

Behind the continuing preoccupation with deer, of course, lay economics, and it would be disingenuous to minimize the reality of the deer's economic significance, either in the Adirondacks or in other areas where it is a major big game species. Nationwide, the hunting of white-tailed deer, when licences, equipment, lodging, and other expenditures are accounted for, constitutes a multi-billion dollar industry. A 1975 survey indicated 12,403,000 deer hunters in the United States, and each of these men and women spent an average of $36 on each hunting day. Deer experts William and RuthAnn Hesselton calculated that the monetary value of a white-tail legally killed in the United States in 1975 was roughly $1,250. It is probably double that today. In 1985 hunters in the northern zone of New York, which includes the Adirondacks, reported 15,422 legal kills. The contribution to the local economy of the thousands of deer hunters who travel to the Adirondacks every fall is enormous.

On the other hand, the damage perpetrated by deer on forestry and agriculture has not been adequately figured. Agricultural products threatened by deer include corn, alfalfa, apples, grapes, buckwheat, and garden vegetables. Even more important in the Adirondacks, deer can prevent the regeneration of those tree species on which they feed, including maples, white cedar, white pine, and hemlock. As the Hesseltons observe,

> Timber growers throughout North America are very much concerned with the problem of deer over-population. Not only do deer retard growing trees, but their selection of certain browse species affects the species composition of trees that grow to maturity. Unquestionably, then, white-tails can and do have tremendous negative impacts that probably collectively amount to hundreds of millions, if not billions of dollars annually.

Limiting the potential for damage to forests is, in fact, yet another way in which deer hunting helps the Adirondack economy. If the thousands of deer taken annually by hunters were not harvested, the degradation of the forest would be much greater. Of course, the relationship between the deer and the harvestable trees they damage is circular: logging operations promote the deer, which in turn feed on commercially valuable species of trees.

* * *

Throughout the 1950s, the conservation bureaucracy pushed the wildlife issue, insisting that the interests of New York hunters would be best served by opening up the Forest Preserve to habitat management of some sort. Because of this and other apparent threats to the integrity of the Forest Preserve (most alarming was the threat of massive development of privately owned forested areas for vacation homes), Governor Nelson Rockefeller established the Temporary Study Commission on the Future of the Adirondacks in 1968. Among the experts invited to submit Technical Reports to the Commission was C. H. D. Clarke, a Canadian wildlife biologist. Dr. Clarke's report is a comprehensive study of the condition of wildlife in the Adirondacks. It also contains bold suggestions for the future, chiefly involving reintroducing extirpated species.

Most of Clarke's suggestions concerned what he believed to be the optimum goals of any state wildlife policy. A hunter himself, Clarke nonetheless argued forcefully against the continuance of a policy calculated almost exclusively to produce deer, to put them, as he expressed it, "before the gun." The wildlife community that the state should strive to achieve in the Adirondacks, Clarke asserted, should represent historical reality, and it should require a minimum of management or intervention. As a model for Adirondack wildlife policy, Clarke proposed the Report of the Advisory Board on Wildlife Management in National Parks, produced in the 1960s and widely known as the Leopold Report, after its chief author A. Starker Leopold.

The most important recommendation of this report, which Clarke submitted should be applied to the Adirondacks as well, was that "the biotic associations within each park be maintained, or where necessary recreated, as nearly as possible in the condition that prevailed when the area was first visited by the white man. A national park should represent a vignette of primitive America." If rigorously pursued in the Adirondacks, Clarke admitted, such a policy would "demand that deer be prevented from dominating the vegetation. In the long run deer numbers would be reduced by establishing a forest of big mature trees such as once stood, when there were more moose and less deer than now."

In other words, Clarke advised the state's wildlife policy makers to aim for a wildlife community that was historically representative:

> My own choice of environment would be that of the early days of penetration, when the aura of romance was first acquired. There was a magnificent diversity of human activities, but there was also a magnificent wildness, stands of beautiful trees, and a rich variety of wildlife, including wilderness species. . . . In any [plan for restoring this environment] wildlife interests should be strongly represented, because wildlife is more than anything else the hallmark of quality.

The critical point in Clarke's vision for the future is the preference for variety over abundance. A wilderness environment, he maintained, offered more species but fewer total animals than a forest managed to produce deer. Bring back the moose, the wolf, the mountain lion, the wolverine, he recommended, and let the deer population decrease to numbers which the range can viably support and which are more faithful to the size of the deer herd early in the nineteenth century.

In the last twenty years or so, the New York Department of Environmental Conservation has departed, to a degree, from its historic obsession with deer. Given the limits on effective deer management inscribed in the constitution, it cannot do much to promote deer anyway. A concern with just the sort of issues advanced by Clarke, moreover, has become increasingly significant in official wildlife policy. The precise extent of this shift in goals is difficult to measure. A 1992 statement on "Our Values" issued by the Division of Fish and Wildlife declared that assuring "human use of fish and wildlife, including observation, study, hunting, fishing and trapping" continues to be its primary objective. But the same document also recognized an obligation to "manage and perpetuate a healthy and diverse assemblage of fish, wildlife and ecosystems." To this latter end, the DEC has devoted energy and resources to the successful restoration of bald eagles and peregrine falcons to the Park. And DEC biologists have been closely involved with plans to restore extirpated mammals, especially moose, to their former range.

* * *

Among biologists there is some disagreement over whether a reintroduction of moose would succeed. Clarke believed that in certain parts of the Forest Preserve the deer population had declined to levels approximately comparable to those in Ontario where moose still live, and he argued that a reintroduction attempt might be successful. He suggested that a few moose be secured, possibly from New Brunswick, placed in a wild area with a low deer population, and prevented from moving around for a while by an enclosure, perhaps an electrified fence. Once the moose had become accustomed to their new home, the fence could be removed. He did not indicate how the cost of such a project could be covered.

Recent research has shown that the possibility for successful reintroduction of moose into a range where deer are already living involves more than simply the numbers of deer. While it remains clear that *P. tenuis* infects both white-tailed deer and moose, other important factors must be considered. For one thing, *P. tenuis* requires an intermediate host species, certain snails, where it lives before being picked up by a browsing deer or moose. The population of these snails, in turn, largely depends on the moisture and quality of the soil. In a forest growing on dry, sandy soil, the snail population is minimal, and deer and moose can successfully coexist. Other factors crucial to the survival of moose are the availability of browse, aquatic vegetation, and suitable wintering range. Even where moose are infested with *P. tenuis*, moreover, it is possible for births to overcome the mortality attributable to the brain disease. The evidence supporting the possibility of successfully returning moose to the Adirondacks seems to be growing.

And while the biologists have argued with each other, the moose has come back to the Adirondacks without human assistance. Beginning in the late 1970s, several moose wandered into the region, possibly from Ontario or from northern New England, where moose populations have been

A radio-collared moose browses in the central Adirondacks.
Photo by Nancie Battaglia.

increasing. They have survived several years of apparent association with white-tailed deer and have thus far not displayed signs of the brain disease. They are being closely watched by state wildlife experts, who are often reluctant to say exactly where these moose have established themselves.

"THE HALLMARK OF QUALITY"

For, despite the fact that the moose is a legally protected species in New York, their greatest enemy may be eager hunters.

The moose taking up residence in the Adirondacks during the 1980s were the subject of an intensive study conducted by Dale Garner, a graduate student in wildlife biology at the State University College of Environmental Science and Forestry at Syracuse University. Garner was based at the Huntington Wildlife Forest, a research station operated by Syracuse near Newcomb. Whenever a moose was reported (the Newcomb facility established a twenty-four hour "moose hot line"), Garner tried to track it down. If he found it, he temporarily immobilized it with a safe muscle-relaxing dart and then checked its sex, age, and health. He also took blood and stool samples for later laboratory work and gave it a dose of antibiotics. The next step involved putting a radio collar on the moose, which, once the moose was up and active again, enabled Garner to monitor its movements, size of range, habitat use patterns, and possible mortality. The entire procedure took fifteen to twenty minutes.

In 1987, Garner estimated that from fifteen to thirty moose were living in the Adirondacks. The ratio of males to females was roughly four to one, and there were reports of about five calves, although Garner did not know whether they were born, or, equally important, conceived, in the Adirondacks. A pregnant cow may have wandered into the Adirondacks and delivered her calf here. The question of whether or not the moose in the Adirondacks are breeding is critical. We cannot claim to have a resident population until evidence of successful breeding is clear.

And according to Garner, we will not have a breeding population until we have a better male-female ratio, ideally one to one. The moose that have migrated to the Adirondacks have probably done so because of increasing populations in Ontario or northern New England, and males are more likely to migrate than females. In order for the Adirondack moose to have a better chance for permanent reestablishment, argues Garner, we need more females. Transplants have been successful elsewhere, recently in Michigan, for example, where twenty-nine imported cows produced twenty-seven calves, and Garner believes a similar project would work here.

The Adirondack environment is ready for moose. Moose can live more successfully than deer can in a closed-canopy forest (though both deer and moose prefer a forest of trees in various stages of succession). The deer population in much of the Forest Preserve is at a level commensurate with coexistence with moose. The browse conditions are suitable. Now that the wolf is gone, no species other than humans offers a significant predatory threat (though black bears may take an occasional calf). Most important, much of the public wants moose in the Adirondacks. Garner reported widespread interest in his research. People called him with moose sightings, and he received letters from all over the state. New Yorkers of all persuasions are fascinated with the idea of the moose's return. They want to help and they are hopeful for the future. Another Adirondack wildlife biologist reported that hunters were protecting the moose known to be inhabiting private preserves.

In June, 1992, the New York State Department of Environmental Conservation issued an Environmental Impact Statement on "Restoration of Moose in Northern New York State." The primary authors of this document, Alan Hicks and Edwin McGowan, begin by noting the unplanned return of moose to part of its historic range and hopefully predict, "Although moose are still few in number, the likelihood of this being a permanent return increases with each passing year." The authors identify several factors in the Adirondacks that appear promising: the Adirondacks offer an environment similar to that of many other regions where moose live; since 1980 no moose in the Adirondacks is known to have been infected by $P.\ tenuis$; and deer densities in the Adirondacks are lower than those in parts of Michigan where moose have been successfully reintroduced.

With these considerations in mind, Hicks and McGowan recommend that 100 moose, 60 cows and 40 bulls, be released in the Adirondacks over a five-year period. Within twenty years, these moose, along with those that have already wandered into the region, would reproduce to a population of some 1300 animals, spread through the fourteen counties of northern New York and concentrated within the Adirondack Park. The cost of the project is estimated at $1,300,000.

> The principal benefit of having moose is the enjoyment people derive from their presence. This includes the pleasures of seeing moose or of anticipating an encounter in moose country. People also appreciate knowing that moose are in New York even though they may never expect to see one. They are gratified in having their state connected with the great northern wilderness with which moose are associated.

Further advantages would eventually accrue, including increased tourism for the region and "the opportunity for regulated recreational hunting."

Potential negative consequences include the impact of moose on agriculture, the possible deleterious effect of moose on the forest-products industry, and the virtual inevitability of automobile accidents involving moose. Of these, only the latter appears at all significant to Hicks and McGowan, who investigated the frequency and seriousness of such accidents in a number of regions where moose populate areas penetrated or surrounded by highways. If moose are restored to the Adirondacks in the numbers recommended, accidents undoubtedly will occur, but they will be rare. Even with the peak population of 1300 moose, the average driver on an Adirondack highway would be ten times more likely to hit a bicyclist than a moose. Nonetheless, when the DEC held public hearings on moose restoration during the summer of 1992, many local residents argued against such a project, citing in particular their fears of increased danger on the highways.

There are other considerations. Much as I want to see a thriving moose population in the Adirondacks, I have reservations about reintroduction. We should remember what happened with the elk and moose the last time we tried something like this. We may not have all the information we need. Snatching an animal from its home and plopping it down in an unfamiliar place is an act of anthropocentric cruelty. Do the proposed benefits, which are by no means certain, justify taking chances with the lives of healthy moose? All signs are that the moose are here to stay. Perhaps we should leave them alone and hope for the best.

* * *

Aside from the moose, the other species around which reintroduction speculation has centered are wolves, lynx, and mountain lions. As with the moose, the key to the reestablishment of wolves is the extent of wilderness. Clarke believed that a large enough, contiguous piece of wild land where wolves could live relatively unaffected by humans was available. And some Adirondackers insist that the wolf never left. Writing in *Adirondack Life*, Bill McKibben reported conversations with local trappers who claimed to have seen and even trapped wolves. But biologists nearly always respond that these are strays and that there is no evidence of a resident population.

In the United States, the eastern timber wolf, a subspecies of the wolf that once inhabited most of North America, currently lives only in Minnesota, Michigan, and Wisconsin. Of these only a relative handful live outside northern Minnesota. Throughout its current range, the eastern timber wolf is classified as threatened by the U. S. Fish and Wildlife Service, which is interested in reestablishing the wolf in other parts of its former territory. One important reason for expanding the wolf's (or any other rare and endangered species's) range is the need to prevent total extinction caused by an unanticipated local catastrophe, like disease. Among the few sites the Fish and Wildlife Service selected as suitable for reintroduction is the Adirondacks (others are eastern Maine and northwestern Maine and adjacent parts of New Hampshire).

The Fish and Wildlife Service has identified five factors critical to successful wolf restoration: (1) large tracts of wilderness where the human presence is minimal; (2) "ecologically sound management"; (3) "availability of adequate wild prey," chiefly ungulates and beaver; (4) "adequate understanding of wolf ecology"; and (5) keeping disease and parasites under control. Particularly in a restricted range, disease and parasites can threaten a population, and Fish and Wildlife Services biologists are concerned that heartworm, canine parvovirus, and Lyme disease all pose new hazards to the already endangered eastern wolf.

If wolves are to live again in the Adirondacks, they will have to be imported. Whether any such transplanted wolves would stay put or wander off is hard to say. At the present there is no way of knowing for sure what they would do, but Clarke suggested that the best chances of success would depend on acquiring a mated pair with the bitch in whelp. As an initial experiment one pair, equipped with collars containing radio transmitters, could be released. If they did not stray out of the Adirondacks, additional pairs could be released. Jamie Sayen and Michael J. Kellett, of Preserve Appalachian Wilderness, have an intriguing suggestion: Animal Damage Control authorities in Minnesota are currently trapping and killing wolves that appear to prey on domestic animals. Even though the wolf is a protected species there, some ninety wolves were killed in 1990 and another sixty in 1991. Why not bring them to the areas already identified as potential restoration zones, including the Adirondacks, and set them loose? Their chances of survival are by no means certain, but these wolves are trapped to be executed. They have a better chance here than they do in Minnesota.

Besides the natural obstacles—lack of wilderness, problems of relocation—there is also the problem of widespread human hostility toward wolves. Before the Department of Environmental Conservation could entertain the possibility of restoring wolves to the Adirondacks, an extensive program of public education would be necessary. Many people still believe that wolves attack humans and would pose a hazard for campers and hikers. In recent years when various false reports have radiated out of the Adirondacks about the supposed killing or sighting of a wolf, the conservation bureaucracy has received letters from concerned New Yorkers inquiring whether it was safe to take a vacation in the region. Friends of the wolf must work to dispel old myths.

More important, hunters will assume that wolf predation will threaten the Adirondack deer herd. Clarke and other authorities argue that wolves would probably have no lasting effect. But wolves do prey on deer, hunters will point out; therefore, they may further insist, after wolves are introduced, there will be fewer deer. The notion that the deer preyed on by wolves are usually old or sick and thus a burden on the range must be accepted by the public, particularly hunters. McKibben reported widespread local opposition to the possibility of restoring wolves, all based on the assumption that wolves would present unacceptable pressure to a deer population already dwindling as logging activity decreases.

In Ontario, where the issue was not reintroduction but simply protection, conservationists discovered, in addition to the expected hostility from people still adhering to old myths, a positive, nourishing sympathy for wolves. In Algonquin Provincial Park, a favorite vacation experience is listening to the nighttime howl of the rare, but protected (in the Park) wolf. Likewise, in Minnesota, surveys of public attitudes found that two thirds of those interviewed wanted wolves in their state and saw the wolf as an indispensable symbol "of the beauty and wonder of nature." All across North America in recent years the wolf has been the focus of considerable research and publicity. If wolves were restored to the Adirondacks, they would quickly acquire a state-wide constituency, eager to protect and promote their presence here.

As for the mountain lion (referred to by many writers as puma or cougar), although the last documented Adirondack mountain lion was killed in 1894, some authorities believe that it has never been completely extirpated from the region. Hardly any biologist will say for certain that no mountain lion lives in the Adirondacks. The mountain lion by habit and nature is different from the wolf (for one thing, mountain lions live and hunt alone) and could possibly have survived. There have been reports of sightings throughout this century. In 1972 a man saw a large cat in the forest near Indian Lake and managed to take its picture; this photograph was subsequently confirmed as a genuine picture of a mountain lion. In 1985, I was driving on route 30 just east of Indian Lake when a mountain lion crossed the road in front of my car. I have been studying the mountain lion (in, I admit, a bookish way) for twenty years, and I am certain that the cat I saw was a mountain lion. In the late 1980s several sightings occurred at Whitney Park. Evidence of mountain lions in the Adirondacks is routinely reported to the Department of Environmental Conservation.

Indeed, wildlife authorities throughout the eastern United States and Canada have recorded over a thousand sightings in the last decade. John Lutz, founder of the Eastern Puma Research Network, told the *New York Times* in 1991, "cougars are out there." He added that although they had been driven from much of their range a century ago, "now they're coming back on an arc from Georgia up to Maine, especially in the Great Smoky Mountains, the Catskills, the Adirondacks and the White Mountains."

However reliable these reports or evidence of occasional sightings may be, the existence of a breeding population remains problematical. Wildlife biologists distinguish between strays or released animals and genuinely resident ones. And the chief measure of a truly resident species is whether it breeds and reproduces. Establishing proof of a breeding population of

Lynx from the Yukon awaiting release in the High Peaks.
Photo by Nancie Battaglia.

mountain lions in the Adirondacks would be supremely difficult. Short of finding a den with newly born kittens in it, it is hard to imagine precisely what would constitute conclusive evidence. In the meantime, the odd, and brief, sighting of a great tawny cat bounding across the path and disappearing into the woods reminds us of the diverse Adirondack wildlife that once existed.

Reintroduction would be unpredictable. Less research has been done on mountain lions than on wolves, and it is hard to say what a transplanted mountain lion would do upon finding itself in the middle of the Adirondacks. Furthermore, anyone trying to reestablish mountain lions would have a difficult time securing suitable specimens for release. Care should be taken not to release a subspecies significantly different from the mountain lions that originally inhabited the Adirondacks, such as the larger cats in the American West. Perhaps one or two could be obtained in Ontario or New Brunswick, but even there the population of mountain lions is dubious. Even if they could be found, Canadian authorities, no doubt, would resist their removal. Probably the best hope for the Adirondack mountain lion is that it might still be around and that if it is it can be rigorously protected.

Every few years a lynx turns up in the Adirondacks, but despite Clarke's hopes that a residual population has survived here, the lynx appears to be extirpated in New York State. Trying to restore this cat, biologists at the Huntington Wildlife Forest undertook an experimental release program, beginning with the release of five lynx in January of 1989. Eventually some eighty-three lynx, all acquired in the Yukon, were released in the High Peaks. They quickly dispersed over an incredibly wide area. With no sense of home territory, they wandered far from the release site, with one (they were all equipped with radio collars and identifying information) showing up as far away as Maryland. Others appeared throughout New England and in eastern Canada. Many of the lynx began hunting along roadsides and were killed by cars: a state biologist remarked, "It looks like the automobile is going to be the lynx's major predator." Although a few of the imported lynx may have survived and reproduced, no hard evidence indicates that this has been a successful project. Like the attempt to introduce elk to the region early this century, the lynx experience suggests that moving wild animals from one place to another should be done rarely if at all and then with humility, reverence, and great caution.

* * *

If Clarke is correct—and obviously I think he is—that wildlife is the environmental "hallmark of quality," then New Yorkers have a rare opportunity in the Adirondacks. An environment capable of sustaining its historic wildlife species either exists or is close to existing: the return of the moose suggests that we may closer than even Clarke thought just over two decades ago. The State Land Master Plan, adopted in 1972, largely as a result of the work performed by the Temporary Study Commission on the Future of the Adirondacks, governs policy for and management of the Adirondack Forest

Preserve. This document and virtually all official decisions regarding the Forest Preserve over the past twenty years show that New York State is committed to protecting and enhancing wilderness in the Adirondacks.

The definition of wilderness in the Master Plan contains important implications for wildlife. Based on the definition of wilderness in the 1964 Federal Wilderness Act, it affirms that a wilderness "is hereby recognized as an area where the earth and its community of life are untrammeled by man." Wilderness, according to this line of thinking, involves more than vast areas of forest unpenetrated by roads and protected from other human intrusions. It also possesses a "community of life," and wildlife values thus constitute an important focus for wilderness managers. Wilderness, in addition to being a place for human recreation or spiritual renewal, is wildlife habitat. And it is home for its wildlife all the time. People come only as visitors.

In a textbook written for classes on wilderness management, Clarence A. Schoenfeld and John C. Hendee have established a list of objectives concerning wildlife in wilderness areas. Although they had federal wilderness in mind, these goals seem particularly applicable to the Adirondacks:

> To seek natural distributions, numbers, and interactions of indigenous species of wildlife.
>
> To the greatest extent possible, to allow natural processes to control Wilderness ecosystems and their wildlife.
>
> To keep wildlife wild, their behavior altered as little as possible by human influences.
>
> To permit viewing, hunting, and fishing where such activities are (1) biologically sound, (2) legal, and (3) conducted in the spirit of the Wilderness experience.
>
> Whenever appropriate, to favor the preservation of those rare, threatened, and endangered species dependent on Wilderness conditions.
>
> Within the constraints of transcending legislation applicable to wildlife in a particular Wilderness, to seek the least possible degradation of the qualities that make for Wilderness—naturalness, solitude, and absence of permanent visible evidence of human activity.

These objectives supply a useful blueprint for what we can aim for in the Adirondacks. They mean returning, where it is scientifically and morally sound, those species formerly indigenous, restoring the historical relations between competing or conflicting species, and encouraging a wildlife community that reflects the conditions of the early nineteenth century.

"THE HALLMARK OF QUALITY"

Conservationists in the Adirondacks have come a long way in the last century. Moving from a utilitarian concern about watershed to an interest in wilderness for its recreational and spiritual attributes, they now advance the concept of the ecosystem, the preservation of which must become our ultimate goal. In wilderness we have a special kind of ecosystem, one where natural processes govern, and where management is largely passive. Any ecosystem that does not support indigenous species in a reasonable approximation of their relative numbers at the time before white contact simply fails the wilderness standard. In the Adirondacks, the key missing element is an ecosystem sufficiently extensive to support these original inhabitants. The big predators, eastern timber wolves and mountain lions, need wild country in large chunks. The state must consolidate and expand the Forest Preserve.

New York has declared its intention to protect wilderness in the Adirondacks. It has, moreover, defined wilderness in a way that requires support, respect, and protection for native species. If New York is to fulfill its self-imposed mandate to provide wilderness for its people, then it must constantly be sensitive to the wildlife in the areas designated as wilderness. Clarke's report of two decades ago remains the single best vision of the possible. The Commission on the Adirondacks in the Twenty-First Century could add nothing to it, recommending simply that "Wildland and wildlife in the Park should be managed to foster the Adirondack environment and all the flora and fauna historically associated with it." Clarke's picture of an environment characterized by quality, variety, and historical authenticity must be one of the chief measurements of the success of any efforts to protect and enhance wilderness in the Adirondacks. Trees without wildlife are not even a forest. With wildlife they can be a wilderness.

Sources

Aber, Ted, and Stella King. *A History of Hamilton County.* Lake Pleasant, NY: Great Wilderness Books, 1965.
Adirondack Council. "Adirondack Wildlife—The Hallmark of Quality." *The Adirondack Council Newsletter*, 8 (July 1983).
Aprill, Dennis. "Will Deer Survive?" *Adirondack Life*, 18 (Jan-Feb 1987).
Benedict, F.N. "The Wilds of Northern New York." *Putnam's Magazine*, 4 (Sept. 1854).
Bradford, William. *Of Plymouth Plantation, 1620-1647.* Samuel E. Morison, ed. New York: Knopf, 1952.
Cartier, Jacques. *A Short and Brief Narration of the Two Navigations and Discoveries to the Northwest Partes Called Newe Fraunce.* London: H. Bynneman, 1580.
Champlain, Samuel de. *Voyages of Samuel de Champlain, 1604-1618.* W. L. Grant, ed. New York: C. Scribner's Sons, 1907.
"Champlain's Expedition." *Documentary History of New York.* Vol. 3. E. B. O'Callaghan, ed. Albany: Weed, Parsons, 1850-51.
Chapman, Joseph A., and George A. Feldhamer, eds. *Wild Mammals of North America: Biology, Management, and Economics.* Baltimore and London: The Johns Hopkins Univ. Press, 1982.
Chase, Greenleaf T. "The Bear Facts." *New York State Conservationist*, 9 (Oct.-Nov. 1954).
Clarke, C. H. D. "Wildlife." *The Future of the Adirondacks: The Technical Reports.* Blue Mountain Lake, NY: Adirondack Museum, 1972.
Coady, John. "Moose." *Wild Mammals of North America.* Joseph A. Chapman and George A. Feldhamer, eds. Baltimore and London: The Johns Hopkins Univ. Press, 1982.
Colvin, Verplanck. *Report on a Topographical Survey of the Adirondack Wilderness of New York.* Albany: Weed, Parsons, 1873.

_____. *Seventh Annual Report on the Progress of the Topographical Survey of the Adirondack Region of New York, to the Year 1879, Containing the Condensed Reports for the Years 1874-75-76-77 and 78.* Albany: Weed, Parsons, 1880.

Commission on the Adirondacks in the Twenty-First Century. *The Adirondack Park in the Twenty-First Century*. [Albany]: State of New York, 1990.

Conservation Commission. *Annual Reports*. 1911-1926.

Conservation Department. *Annual Reports*. 1927-1969.

Cronon, William. *Changes in the Land: Indians, Colonists, and the Ecology of New England*. New York: Hill and Wang, 1983.

Cutright, Paul Russell. *Theodore Roosevelt: The Making of a Conservationist*. Urbana and Chicago: University of Illinois Press, 1985.

Davis, George. *Adirondack Council, State of the Park—1985*. Elizabethtown: Adirondack Council, 1985.

_____. *Man and the Adirondack Environment: a Primer*. Blue Mountain Lake, NY: Adirondack Museum, 1977.

_____. *A Special Report: State of the Park 1986*. Elizabethtown: Adirondack Council, 1986.

DeKay, James E. *Zoology of New York; Or, the New York Fauna*. 2 vols. Albany: Carroll and Cook, 1842-44.

DiNunzio, Michael G. *Adirondack Wildguide: A Natural History of the Adirondack Park*. Elizabethtown, NY: Adirondack Conservancy Committee and Adirondack Council, 1984.

Division of Fish and Wildlife, New York State Department of Environmental Conservation. "Memorandum, Revised Values and Mission Statements." 14 December 1992.

Donaldson, Alfred Lee. *A History of the Adirondacks*. 2 vols. New York: Century, 1921.

Dunlap, Thomas R. "American Wildlife Policy and Environmental Ideology: Poisoning Coyotes, 1939-1972." *Pacific Historical Review*, 55 (Aug. 1986).

Durant, Kenneth, and Helen Durant. *The Adirondack Guide-Boat*. Camden Maine: International Marine Publishing Co., 1980.

Dwight, Timothy. *Travels in New-England and New-York*. 4 vols. New Haven: S. Converse, 1821.

Ekirch, Arthur A. Jr. *Man and Nature in America*. New York: Columbia Univ. Press, 1963.

Emerson, Ralph Waldo. "The Adirondacs: A Journal Dedicated to My Fellow Travellers in August, 1858." *May-Day and Other Pieces*. Boston: Ticknor and Fields, 1867.

"Evicted Tenants of the Adirondacks." *Harper's Weekly*, 29 (28 Feb. 1885).

First St. Lawrence University Conference on the Adirondacks. *Proceedings*. Canton, NY: St. Lawrence Univ., 1970.

Fisheries, Game, Forest Commission. *Annual Reports*. 1895-1899.
Forest and Stream. 1873-1930.
Forest, Fish and Game Commission. *Annual Reports*. 1900-1910.
Forest Commission. *Annual Reports*. 1885-1894.
Fosburgh, Pieter W. "Editorial." *New York State Conservationist,* 6 (Oct.-Nov.1951).
_____. "Panther." *New York State Conservationist*, 5 (June-July, 1951).
Fox, William F. "History of the Lumber Industry in the State of New York." New York Forest, Fish and Game Commission. *6th Annual Report* (Albany: Weed Parsons, 1901).
Fugazi, Linda. "The Mysterious Eastern Coyote: Old Wolf or New Predator?" *Adirondac*, 50 (July 1986).
Gilborn, Craig. *Durant: The Fortunes and Woodland Camps of a Family in the Adirondacks*. Sylvan Beach, NY: North Country Books, 1981.
Graham, Frank Jr. *The Adirondack Park: A Political History*. New York: Knopf, 1978.
Grant, T. Madison. "Adirondack Moose." New York Forest, Fish and Game Commission. *Sixth Annual Report.* Albany: Weed, Parsons, 1901.
_____. "Notes on Adirondack Mammals." New York Forest, Fish and Game Commission. *Eighth and Ninth Annual Reports*. Albany: Weed, Parsons, 1902-03.
Grondahl, Paul. "Missing Lynx." *Albany Times-Union*, 29 November 1992.
Guthe, Carl E. "The Indian Hunter." *New York State Conservationist*, 2 (Oct.-Nov., 1947).
Hallock, Charles. "The Raquette Club." *Harper's Magazine*, 41 (Aug. 1870).
Hammond, Samuel H. *Hills, Lakes and Forest Streams*. New York: J. C. Derby, 1854.
_____. *Wild Northern Scenes*. New York: Derby and Jackson, 1857.
Hays, Samuel P. *Conservation and the Gospel of Efficiency: The Progressive Conservation Movement, 1890-1920*. Reprint. New York: Atheneum, 1969.
Headley, Joel T. *The Adirondack; or, Life in the Woods*. New York: Baker and Scribner, 1849.
Hesselton, William T., and Ruth-Ann Monson Hesselton. "White-tailed Deer." *Wild Mammals of North America*. Joseph A. Chapman and George A. Feldhamer, eds. Baltimore and London: The Johns Hopkins Univ. Press, 1982.
Hicks, Alan, and Edwin McGowan. *Draft Environmental Impact Statement: Restoration of Moose in Northern New York State*. Delmar, NY: NYS DEC Wildlife Resources Center, 1992.
Hill, Edward P. "Beaver." *Wild Mammals of North America*. Joseph A. Chapman and George A. Feldhamer, eds. Baltimore and London: The Johns Hopkins Univ. Press, 1982.

Hochschild, H. K. *Township 34: A History, With Digressions, of an Adirondack Township in Hamilton County in the State of New York.* New York: Privately Printed, 1952.
Hoffman, Charles Fenno. *Wild Scenes in the Forest and Prairie.* New York: W. H. Colyer, 1843.
Hornaday, William T. *Our Vanishing Wild Life.* New York: Charles Scribner's Sons, 1913.
Hunt, George T. *Wars of the Iroquois.* Madison: Univ. of Wisconsin Press, 1940.
Hurd, D. H. *History of Clinton and Franklin Counties.* Philadelphia: J. W. Lewis, 1880.
Huth, Hans. *Nature and the American: Three Centuries of Changing Attitudes.* Berkeley: Univ. of California Press, 1957.
Jameson, J. Franklin, ed. *Narratives of New Netherland, 1609-1664.* New York: Scribner's, 1909.
Jellisky, Joseph. Unpublished typescript biography of Verplanck Colvin.
Jennings, Virginia. "Cougars in Them There Mountains." *Hamilton County News*, 30 Oct.-5 Nov. 1990.
"Journal of Major Winthrop's March from Albany to Wood Creek." *Documents Relating to the Colonial History of the State of New York.* Vol. 4. E. B. O'Callaghan, ed. Albany: Weed Parsons, 1857-87.
Juet, Robert. "From 'The Third Voyage of Master Henry Hudson,' By Robert Juet, 1610." *Narratives of New Netherland, 1609-1664.* J. Franklin Jameson, ed. New York: Scribner's, 1909.
Kaiser, Harvey H. *Great Camps of the Adirondacks.* Boston: David R. Godine, 1982.
Kalinoski, Tom. "Public Enemy Number One?" *Adirondack Life,* 22 (March-April, 1991).
Kalm, Peter. *Travels in North America.* John Reinhold Forster, trans. Warrington, Eng, 1770.
Kellett, Michael J. "Bring Timber Wolves Back to Maine." Unpublished manuscript.
Ketchledge, E. H. *Trees of the Adirondack High Peak Region.* Gabriels, NY: Adirondack Mountain Club, 1967.
Kranz, Marvin Wolf. "Pioneering in Conservation." Ph.D. Dissertation. Syracuse University, 1961.
Laet, Johan de. "From the 'New World,' By Johan de Laet, 1625, 1630, 1633, 1640." *Narratives of New Netherland, 1609-1664.* J. Franklin Jameson, ed. New York: Scribner's, 1909.
LaHontan, Louis Armand de Lom d'Arce, Baron de. *New Voyages to North America.* Reuben Gold Thwaites, ed. Chicago: A. C. McClurg, 1905.
Lanman, Charles. *Adventures of an Angler in Canada, Nova Scotia, and the United States.* London: Richard Bentley, 1848.

SOURCES

Laws of New York.

Leopold, A. Starker (Chairman). *Reports of the Special Advisory Board on Wildlife Management for the Secretary of the Interior 1963-1968.* Washington: Wildlife Management Institute, 1969.

Leopold, Aldo. *A Sand County Almanac and Sketches Here and There.* New York: Oxford University Press, 1949.

Lopez, Barry Holstun. *Arctic Dreams: Imagination and Desire in a Northern Landscape.* New York: Scribners, 1986.

_____. *Of Wolves and Men.* New York: Scribners, 1978.

Lossing, Benson J. *The Hudson: From the Wilderness to the Sea.* New York: Virtue and Yorston, 1866.

Lundy, John P. *The Saranac Exiles.* Philadelphia: privately printed, 1880.

Lyons, Richard D. "Outdoors: Sighting the 'Extinct' Eastern Cougar." *New York Times*, 1 April 1991.

McCord, Chet M., and James E. Cardoza. "Bobcat and Lynx." *Wild Mammals of North America.* Joseph A. Chapman and George A. Feldhamer, eds. Baltimore and London: The Johns Hopkins Univ. Press, 1982.

McKibben, Bill. "The Return of a Native." *Adirondack Life*, 19 (May/June 1988).

Martin, Calvin. *Keepers of the Game: Indian-Animal Relationships and the Fur Trade.* Berkeley: Univ. of California Press, 1978.

Masten, Arthur H. *The Story of Adirondac.* New York: Privately printed, 1923.

_____. *Tahawus Club, 1898-1933.* Burlington, VT: Free Press, 1935.

Mech, L. David. *The Wolf.* Garden City, NY: American Museum of Natural History, 1970.

Megapolensis, Johannes. "A Short Account of the Mohawk Indians, By Reverend Johannes Megapolensis, Jr., 1644." *Narratives of New Netherland, 1609-1664.* J. Franklin Jameson, ed. New York: Scribner's, 1909.

Merriam, C. Hart. *The Mammals of the Adirondack Region, Northeastern New York.* New York: Privately printed, 1884.

Mitchell, Lee Clark. *Witnesses to a Vanishing America: The Nineteenth Century.* Princeton: Princeton Univ. Press, 1981.

Montanus, Arnoldus. "Description of New Netherland, 1671." *Documentary History of New York.* Vol. 4. E. B. O'Callaghan, ed. Albany: Weed, Parsons, 1850-51.

Morison, Samuel Eliot. *The European Discovery of America: The Northern Voyages.* New York: Oxford University Press, 1971.

_____. *Samuel de Champlain: Father of New France.* Boston: Little, Brown, 1972.

Morse, Jedidiah. *The American Gazetteer.* London: Reprinted for J. Stockdale, 1798.

Murray, William Henry Harrison. *Adventures in the Wilderness; or, Camp-Life in the Adirondacks*. Boston: Fields, Osgood, and Co., 1869; reprint, Blue Mountain Lake and Syracuse: Adirondack Museum and Syracuse Univ. Press, 1970.

Nash, Roderick. *Wilderness and the American Mind*. 3rd ed. New Haven: Yale Univ. Press, 1983.

"New York's Clever Coyotes." *New York Times*, 25 September 1991.

O'Callaghan, E. B., ed. *The Documentary History of the State of New-York*. 4 vols. Albany: Charles Van Benthuysen, 1851-52.

_____. *Documents Relative to the Colonial History of the State of New-York*. 12 vols. Albany: Weed, Parsons, 1853-87.

Parkman, Francis. *The Oregon Trail: Being Sketches of Prairie and Rocky Mountain Life*. Boston: George Putnam, 1849.

Paradiso, John L., and Ronald Nowak. "Wolves." *Wild Mammals of North America*. Joseph A. Chapman and George A. Feldhamer, eds. Baltimore and London: The Johns Hopkins Univ. Press, 1982.

Pelton, Michael R. "Black Bear." *Wild Mammals of North America*. Joseph A. Chapman and George A. Feldhamer, eds. Baltimore and London: The Johns Hopkins Univ. Press, 1982.

Petersen, Allen. "A Brief Report on the Historic Status of the Bison, Elk, Moose in New York State." Typescript of Report prepared for Endangered Species Unit of New York State Department of Environmental Conservation, August 1979.

Phillips, Paul Chrisler. *The Fur Trade*. Norman: Univ. of Oklahoma Press, 1961.

Plum, Dorothy A. *The Adirondack Bibliography*. Gabriels, NY: The Adirondack Mountain Club, 1958.

_____. *The Adirondack Bibliography Supplement, 1956-1965*. Blue Mountain Lake, NY: The Adirondack Museum, 1973.

Pownall, Thomas. *Topographical Description of the Dominions of the United States of America*. Lois Mulkearn, ed. Pittsburgh: Univ. of Pittsburgh Press, 1949.

Radford, Harry. "History of the Adirondack Beaver." *New York State Forest, Fish and Game Commission, Annual Reports for 1904-1905-1906*. Albany: J. B. Lyon, 1908.

Reade, Julian. *Assyrian Sculpture*. London: British Museum, 1983.

Reiger, John F. *American Sportsmen and the Origins of Conservation*. New York: Winchester Press, 1975.

Richards, T. Addison. "A Forest Story." *Harper's New Monthly Magazine*, 19 (June-Nov. 1859).

Ritchie, William A. "The Indian and His Environment." *New York State Conservationist*, (Dec.-Jan., 1955-56).

Robinson, William L., and Eric G. Bolen. *Wildlife Ecology and Management*. New York: Macmillan, 1984.

SOURCES

Rue, Leonard Lee. *The World of the Beaver.* New York: Lippincott, 1964.

Salisbury, Neal. *Manitou and Providence: Indians, Europeans, and the Making of New England, 1500-1643.* New York: Oxford Univ. Press, 1982.

Saunders, D. Andrew. *Adirondack Mammals.* State University of New York College of Environmental Science and Forestry, no date.

Schoenfeld, Clarence A., and John C. Hendee. *Wildlife Management in Wilderness.* Pacific Grove, CA: Boxwood Press, 1978.

Schullery, Paul. " 'A Sportsman's Paradise': Fishing and Hunting on the Preserve." *The Adirondack League Club, 1890-1990.* Edward Comstock, Jr., ed. Old Forge, NY: The Adirondack League Club, 1990.

Severinghaus, C. W., and C. P. Brown. "History of the White-Tailed Deer in New York." *New York Fish and Game Journal,* 3 (July 1956).

Severinghaus, C. W., and L. W. Jackson. "Feasibility of Stocking Moose in the Adirondacks." *New York Fish and Game Journal,* 17 (Jan. 1970).

Simms, J. R. *Trappers of New York; Or, A Biography of Nicholas Stoner and Nathaniel Foster Together with Anecdotes of Other Celebrated Hunters.* Albany: J. Munsell, 1850.

Singleton, Alison. "Study: Can Moose Survive in the Adirondacks?" *Plattsburgh Press-Republican,* March 31, 1987.

Smith, H. Perry. *The Modern Babes in the Wood: or, Summerings in the Wilderness. To Which is Added a Reliable and Descriptive Guide to the Adirondacks. By E. R. Wallace.* Syracuse: Watson Gill, 1872.

Snyder, Charles. "John Brown's Tract." *Papers Read Before the Herkimer County Historical Society During the Years 1896, 1897, and 1898.* Arthur T. Smith, comp. Herkimer: Citizen Publishing Co., 1899.

Street, A. B. *Woods and Waters; or, the Saranacs and Racket.* New York: M. Doolady, 1860.

Stoddard, S. R. *The Adirondacks Illustrated.* Albany: Weed, Parsons, 1874.

Stoner, Dayton. *Extant New York State Specimens of the Adirondack Cougar.* New York State Museum Circular 25; Albany: University of the State of New York, 1950.

Sylvester, Nathaniel. *Historical Sketches of Northern New York and the Adirondack Wilderness.* Troy, NY: William H. Young, 1877.

Terrie, Philip G. "Behind the Blue Line." *Adirondack Life,* 23 (Feb. 1992).

_____. "The Changing Wildlife of the Adirondack Park: The Way Things Were—The Way Things Are." *The Conservationist,* 46 (May-June 1992).

_____. *Forever Wild: Environmental Aesthetics and the Adirondack Forest Preserve.* Philadelphia: Temple University Press, 1985.

_____. "R.I.P.: The Adirondack Moose." *Adirondack Life,* 4 (Fall 1973).

_____. "Urban Man Confronts the Wilderness: The Nineteenth-Century Sportsman in the Adirondacks." *Journal of Sport History,* 5 (Winter 1978).

Thomas, Keith. *Man and the Natural World*. London: Allen Lane, 1983.

Thoreau, Henry David. *The Maine Woods*. Princeton: Princeton University Press, 1972.

Thorpe, Thomas Bangs. "A Visit to 'John Brown's Tract.' " *Harper's New Monthly Magazine*, 19 (June-Nov. 1859).

Todd, John. *Long Lake*. Pittsfield, MA: E. P. Little, 1845.

Trefethen, James B. *An American Crusade for Wildlife*. New York: Winchester Press and Boone and Crockett Club, 1975.

Thwaites, Reuben Gold, ed. *Jesuit Relations*. New York: Pageant Book Co., 1959.

Tober, James A. *Who Owns the Wildlife: The Political Economy of Conservation in Nineteenth-Century America*. Westport, CT: Greenwood Press, 1981.

Trigger, Bruce. *The Children of Aataentsic: A History of the Huron People to 1660*. 2 vols. Montreal and London: McGill-Queens University Press, 1976.

U. S. Fish and Wildlife Service. *Recovery Plan for the Eastern Timber Wolf*. Twin Cities, MN, 1992.

Van der Donck, Adriaen, et al . "The Representation of New Netherland, 1650." *Narratives of New Netherland, 1609-1664*. J. Franklin Jameson, ed. New York: Scribner's, 1909.

VanValkenburgh, Norman J. *The Adirondack Forest Preserve*. Blue Mountain Lake, NY: The Adirondack Museum, 1979.

Vaughn, Kathleen Scott. "DEC Fields Questions from Public on Moving Moose to Ad'ks." *Adirondack Daily Enterprise*, 12 August 1992.

Wallace, E. R. *Descriptive Guide to the Adirondacks and Hand-Book of Travel*. Syracuse: The author, 1881.

Warner, Charles Dudley. *In the Wilderness*. Boston: Houghton, Osgood, 1878.

Watson, Winslow C. *Military and Civil History of the County of Essex, New York*. Albany: J. Munsell, 1869.

Webber, C. W. *Romance of Sporting, Or, Wild Scenes and Wild Hunters*. Philadelphia: J. B. Lippincott, 1852.

White, Lynn. "The Historical Roots of Our Ecological Crisis." *Science*, 155 (10 March 1967).

White, William Chapman. *Adirondack Country*. New York: Knopf, 1954.

Wilson, H. G. "The Beavers of the Adirondacks." *Fur News and Outdoor World*, 36 (Aug 1922).

Woods and Waters, 1898-1906.

Wright, Bruce S. *The Ghost of North America*. New York: Vantage, 1959.

Young, Stanley P. *The Wolves of North America*. New York: Dover, 1944.

_____. *The Puma*. New York: Dover, 1964.

INDEX

Adirondack Club, 118
Adirondack Forest Preserve, 132, 133, 139, 147, 148, 149, 151, 153
Adirondack Game Management District, 141
Adirondack League Club, 90, 91, 106, 116
Adirondack Museum, 8
Adirondack Park, 132, 133
Advisory Board on Wildlife Management in National Parks, 150
Albany Museum, 50
Algonquin Indians, 40
Algonquin Park, 18
American Revolution, 45, 46
Ames, Moses, 76
Ampersand Lake, 68
Animal Damage Control, 156
anthropocentrism, 36, 37, 124
anthropomorphism, 74, 138
Arnold, Ed, 77
Ashurbanipal, 62-63
Averyville, 77
Axton, 93

bald eagles, 151
Bartlett's Hotel, 69
Beach (hermit of Raquette Lake), 58
Beakbane, A. B., 130
Beard, Daniel, 114
beaver, 15, 19, 52, 59; folklore, 33; fur trade, 38-41, 55, 57; restoration of, 128-131, 143-44; scarcity of, 74-75, 93, 115
Bekoff, Marc, 141
Benedict, F. N., 75
Benevolent and Protective Order of Elks, 127-28

Big Blowup of 1951, 148
big horn sheep, 131
Big Moose Lake, 77, 122
black bear, 18, 34, 50, 52, 143; protection of, 108-112; threat to stock, 94, 109
Black River, 28
Blossom, James B., 79
Blowdown, 148
Blue Mountain, 64
boar, 131
bobcat, 19, 55, 93, 142
Bog Lake, 76
Bog River, 64, 75, 78, 116
Boone and Crockett Club, 106
bounties, 18, 54-55, 75, 76, 92-93, 109, 111, 113, 115-16, 140-42
Bradford, William, 32
Bradley Pond, 73
brain disease (moose), 21-22, 118
Brant Lake, 47
British Museum, 62
Brown, C. P., 104
Brown's Tract Guides' Association, 107
Burnham, John, 116, 134

Campbell, Archibald, 14
canopy, forest, 15-16, 20, 133, 147, 153
caribou, 128, 131
Cartier, Jacques, 12, 20, 39
Cary, Reuben, 117
castor (castoreum), 33, 34
Catlin, Linus, 52
Chahoon, George, 109
Champlain, Samuel de, 13, 24, 25, 29, 33, 39, 40, 42, 45,
Champlain Valley, 94, 109

171

Charley's Pond, 77
Charrier, 38
Chateaugay Lake, 73, 100
Cheney, A. N., 115
Cheney, John, 50-53, 55, 58, 63, 70, 74
Clarke, C. H. D., 19, 55, 70, 141, 149, 150, 151, 155, 156, 159, 161
class antagonism, 86-91, 96
climax species, 15
Coady, John W., 16
Cold River, 7, 116
Colvin, Verplanck, 79, 92, 113, 119, 131
Commission on the Adirondacks in the Twenty-First Century, 161
conservation bureaucracy, 9, 133-39, 144-46, 149
Conservation Commission (New York), 127-30, 133-34, 136-39, 143, 144
Conservation Department (New York), 141, 148
Conservation Law, 136
Constable, John and Stevenson, 77
constitution (New York), 21, 91, 132, 133, 139, 144, 148, 150
Cooper, James Fenimore, 46, 51
Couchsachrage, 41
Cox (Forest Commissioner), 131
coyote, 118, 139-42
coypu, 55, 57
Cranberry Lake, 15, 82
Cronon, William, 11, 28, 30
crusting, 85-86, 101
Ctesias, 34
Currier and Ives, 49, 73

Dart, William, 124
Davis, Theodore, 64
DeBar Mountain Game Refuge, 128
de Courcelles (Governor of New France), 43
deer, see white-tailed deer
DeKay, James E., 20 54-5, 56, 57, 58, 74, 92; **Zoology of New York**, 54, 56, 57, 92
de Laet, Johan, 42
Department of Environmental Conservation (New York), 141, 147-48, 150, 151, 154-55, 157; Division of Fish and Wildlife, 151
DeVries, David, 25
Donaldson, Alfred L., 72, 78
Donovan, R. J., 109
driving (deer), Indians, 24-25; early settlers, 48-49, 52-53; sportsmen, 64-65
Dunning, Alvah, 78

Durant, Kenneth and Helen, 72
Durant, Thomas C., 82
Dutch West India Company, 40
Dwight, Timothy, 28, 48, 49, 61

eagles, 32, 151
Eastern Puma Research Network, 157
economics and wildlife, 20, 21, 119, 127, 133, 134, 137, 143, 148
ecosystem, idea of, 161
Eighth Lake, 122
elitism, 88-91
elk, 16, 21, 58-59, 115, 122, 124-28
Emerson, Ralph Waldo, 14
Emmons, Ebenezer, 63
enforcement of game laws, 86-87, 98-102, 104, 107-08, 135-36
ermine 74, 93, 143

farming, 46-47, 57
Federal Wilderness Act, 160
Fenton, Charles, 69, 99, 100
fires, to promote wildlife, 27-28; forest, 47, 95, 104, 117
First Lake, 129
fisher, 19, 55, 75, 93, 142, 143
Fisheries, Game and Forest Commission (New York), 104, 119
Follensby Clear Pond, 67
Follensby Pond, 14
Forest and Stream, 67, 69, 78, 79, 82, 83, 87-90, 91, 97-101, 103, 107, 113, 115-18, 120, 130, 134
Forest Commission (New York), 104
Forest, Fish and Game Commission (New York), 12, 91, 109, 112, 121, 122, 124, 126, 128-29, 135
Forked Lake, 64
Forked Lake Carry, 124
Fort Orange, 42
Foster, Nat, 49, 50, 54
Fourth Lake, 129
fox, 19, 93, 106, 142-43
Fox, Norman and Alanson, 47
Fox, William F., 104-06
Fulton Chain, 46, 76, 82, 88, 129
fur trade, 38-41, 45, 49-50, 55, 57

game dealers, New York City, 103
Garner, Dale, 153-54
Genesis, 37
Glens Falls, 47
"golden calf," 133, 146

INDEX

Graeff, Assemblyman (Essex County), 107
Grant, T. Madison, 78, 112, 115, 124, 131
Great Windfall, 15
Grinnell, George Bird, 106
guideboat, 63, 71-72
guides, 64
Gull Pond, 89

Hallock, Charles, 88
Hammond, Samuel H., 10, 21, 73-77
Hays, Samuel, 138
Headley, Joel T., 50, 52, 55, 58, 59, 66, 68, 69, 81, 83
Hendee, John C., 160
Henderson, David, 58
Hesselton, William and RuthAnn, 16, 148
Hewitt, Steuben, 70
Hicks, Alan, 154
Higgins, Frank W., Governor, 122
hoary bat, 20
Hochelaga, 12
Hochschild, Harold K., 79
Hoffman, Charles Fenno, 50, 53, 58, 63
Holt, Harvey, 58
Homer, Winslow, 51, 108
Honnedaga Lake, 78
Hooper, Assemblyman (Essex County), 131
Hopson, R. E., 116
Hornaday, William T., 112
hounding, 48, 52-53, 64-65, 70-71, 82, 86, 96-100, 102-04, 106-07, 135
Hudson, Henry, 40, 42
Hudson River, 25, 33, 47, 57
hunting, see crusting, driving, hounding, jacking, market hunting, still hunting
Huntington Wildlife Forest, 153, 159
Hurd, D. H., 113
Hurons, 41

Independence Creek, 77
Indian Carry, 64
Indian Lake, 8, 46, 78, 101, 131, 157
Indian Pass, 63
industrialism, 38
Iroquois, 40-44
Ives, Martin Van Buren, 106

jacking, 52, 53, 66, 69-71, 82-86, 96, 98, 102-07
Jesuit Relations, 41
Jock's Lake, 78
Jones, H. Pell, 116
Judaeo-Christianity, 36-38

Kalm, Peter, 44, 45
Kamp Kill Kare, 107
Keene Valley, 46
Kellett, Michael J., 156

Lachine, 39
LaHontan, Baron, 25, 26, 27, 29, 34, 43
Lake Champlain, 27, 33, 44, 50
Lake Clear, 93
Lake George, 45, 48, 49, 70, 108
Lake Kora, 129
Lake Ontario, 24, 43
Lake Placid, 129
Lake Pleasant, 54, 58
Lake Terror, 129
Lanman, Charles, 50, 58, 70, 74, 75
Leopold, Aldo, 8, 116
Leopold, A. Starker, 150
Leopold Report, 150
Lewis, Culver H., 94
Liberty, John, 101
license, hunting, 136, 142
Limekiln Falls, 54
Litchfield, Edward, 129, 131
Litchfield Park, 129
Little Tupper Lake, 76, 77, 124, 129
logging, 13-15, 47, 57, 104, 108, 117, 132-34
Long Island, 57, 97
Long Lake, 46, 54, 58, 64, 74, 76, 111, 127
Long Lake Club, 100
Long Lake guides, 83
Lopez, Barry, 36, 66
Lossing, Benson J., 75, 76
Lower Saranac Lake, 77
Lutz, John, 157
lynx, 19, 55, 93, 142, 159
Lyons Falls, 47

MacDonald, J., 59
Marion River, 79
market hunting, 52, 85, 98-99, 101-03, 105
Marshall, William B., 128
marten, 19, 52, 55, 74, 75, 93, 143
Martin, Calvin, 28, 30, 43, 44, 63
Martin, Charles, 120
Martin's Hotel, 69
Mather, Fred, 78, 88, 113, 115
McGowan, Edwin, 154
McIntyre, Archibald, 58
McIntyre iron mine, 50, 58, 63
McKibben, Bill, 155, 157
Meacham, Thomas, 50
Megapolensis, Johannes, 42

173

Merriam, C. Hart, 20, 58, 77, 85, 91, 92, 93, 95, 113; **The Mammals of the Adirondack Region**, 77, 92, 113
Minerva, 69
mink, 19, 55, 74, 93, 143
Mix, David K., 116
Mohawk River, 23, 28, 40, 42, 97
Mohawk Indians, 42
Montaignais Indians, 41
Montanus, Arnoldus, 32, 33, 34, 35
Montreal, 12
Moody, Harvey, 69, 75, 78
moose, 10, 16, 18, 21, 33, 56, 59; extirpation, 77-80, 95, 115; first restocking, 118-22; hunting, 50, 52, 57-58; return, 147, 150-55
Moose River, 28, 129, 144
Morse, Jedidiah, 46
Mount Colden, 76
Mount Marcy, 58, 63
Mount Seward, 78
mountain goats, 131
mountain lion, 9, 10, 18, 29, 55, 147; attitudes toward, 54; extirpation, 59, 75-76, 92, 113, 115-16, 128; hunting, 50, 52; restocking, 150, 157-59
Mud Lake, 77, 78
Muir, George, 93, 117
Murray, William Henry Harrison, 81-83, 87, 120; **Adventures in the Wilderness**, 81, 84, 87
Murray's Fools, 81, 83, 88, 90
muskrat, 19, 27, 93, 143

narwhal, 35
Native Americans, 23-31
Natty Bumppo, 51
Natural History Survey (New York), 54, 63
Nehasane Park, 91
New Brunswick, 18
New York Association for the Protection of Game, 98, 101
New York Linnæan Society, 92
New York Sportsman's Club, 98
New York State Planning Board, 139
New York Zoological Society, 112
Newcomb, 46, 50, 69, 116, 126, 153
Newcomb Farm, 70
North Creek, 82
North Elba, 77
Northville, 107
nutria, 57

Odell, Benjamin, Governor, 109 111, 121

Ogdensburg, 47
Old Forge, 57, 90, 128, 129
Oswegatchie River, 13, 28, 55
Otis, Stella, 110
otter, 19, 52, 55, 74, 75, 93, 142, 143

Palmer, Ed, 79
Palmer family, 72
Palmer, Sylvester J., 101
Parelaphostrongylus tenuis, 22, 151, 154
Parkman, Francis, 67
Paul Smith's, 124
Pelton, Michael R., 19
peregrine falcons, 151
Pico Lake, 116
Pliny the Elder, 34
Plymouth Plantation, 32
porcupine, 7, 20, 27, 142
Porteous, Andrew, 58
Potsdam, 47
Pownall, Thomas, 41, 44
Preserve Appalachian Wilderness, 156
pygmy shrew, 20

Quebec, 39

raccoon 143
racism, 90-91
Radford, Harry, 19, 93, 109 119-21, 124, 128
Ragged Lake, 73
Raquette Lake, 54, 58, 76, 78, 79, 88, 107, 124
Raquette River, 7, 64, 82
red squirrel, 142
Reiger, John, 67
Remington, Frederick, 68
Richelieu River, 40
Risdon, Elisha, 50
Robertson, W. C., 76
Rock Pond, 77
Roosevelt, Theodore, 106

Sabael, 46
Sabattis, Mitchell, 72, 78
Sacandaga River, 49, 63
Salisbury, Neal, 28
salt lick, 26, 52, 53, 85, 98
Sand Lake, 79
Santa Clara, 93
Saranac Lakes, 46, 64, 69
Saranac River, 58
Sayen, Jamie, 156
Schoenfeld, Clarence A., 160
Schroon River, 47

INDEX

Sears, George Washington (Nessmuk), 88
season, deer, 44-45, 97-98, 100, 103-04, 106-07, 144-46
Seventh Lake Mountain, 77, 92
Severinghaus, C. W., 104
Seward lean-to, 7
Seymour, Adirondack French Louie, 104
Seymour, Horatio, 78
sheep, 54, 94, 109
Simms, Jeptha R., 49
Six Nations, 41
skunk, 143
Smith, Edward Clarence, 79
Smith's Lake, 100
snowshoes, 27, 50, 59, 85
Snyder, Charles, 57
sport hunting, 61-63
sportsmanship, 52, 68, 89
spring mountain lamb, 69
St. Francis of Assisi, 37
St. Lawrence River, 12, 23, 28, 33, 39
St. Regis Indians, 55
St. Regis Lake, 75
St. Regis Pond, 93
St. Regis River, 93
State Land Master Plan, 159-60
State University College of Environmental Science and Forestry, 153
still hunting, 25, 52, 53, 69, 85, 99
Stoddard, Seneca Ray, 105
Stoddard's **Guide**, 82
Stoner, Nick, 49, 50, 54
Stony Creek Ponds, 68
Stony Creek, 64
Street, Alfred Billings, 69, 74, 75, 76, 78
sturgeon, 33
summer shooting, 103, 105, 135

Tahawus Club, 118
Tait, Arthur Fitzwilliam, 60, 61, 79, 86
Taylor, Charles A., 119
Temporary Study Commission on the Future of the Adirondacks, 19, 141, 149, 159
Thendara, 78
Thirteenth Lake, 126
Thorpe, Thomas Bangs, 53
Thoreau, Henry David, 21, 80
Ticonderoga, 47, 50
Todd, John, 74
Tongue Mountain, 126
Totten and Crossfield Purchase, 14
trapping, 49-50, 55, 143-44
Tucker (guide of S. H. Hammond), 10, 76

Tupper Lake, 7, 64, 69, 75, 76, 78, 129

U. S. Fish and Wildlife Service, 155
U. S. Forest Service, 148
Uncas Station, 121, 122
unicorn, 34-36
Upper Saranac Lake, 128

Van der Donck, Adriaen, 27, 33, 34, 41, 42, 43
van Meteren, Emmanuel, 42
Vanderwhacker Mountain, 69

"Wachusett," 81
Wagstaff, State Senator, 118
Wallace's **Guide**, 82, 116
Ward, Spencer, 92
Warner, Charles Dudley, 52
Watson, Winslow C., 75, 79
weasel, 142
Webb, W. Seward, 91, 119, 120
Webber, C. W., 58
Wells, 54, 77
West Canada Creek, 78
West Canada Lake, 104
Whipple, James S., 129
White, Lynn, Jr., 36-38
white-tailed deer, 9, 10, 15-16, 18, 57; and early settlers, 48-53; and Native Americans, 22-27, 29; and sportsmen, 63-74, 82-87; and state wildlife bureaucracy, 133-35, 136-39, 144-46, 147-49; fears concerning decline, 88-89; image of, 60, 74; statutes, 96-107
Whitney, William C., 124
wilderness, 21, 32, 36, 66, 67, 80, 85, 92, 147, 148, 150, 156, 160, 161
wildlife management, 136-39, 160
Wilds, Truman, 77
Winthrop, Major, 13
withing, 52
Withmore, E. T., 83
wolf, 9, 10, 18, 50, 54, 57, 59; extirpation, 113-15, 117-18; persecution of, 75-76, 92, 93; restocking, 147 150, 155-57
wolverine, 10, 19, 27, 54, 93, 115, 150
Wood, Alonzo, 77
Wood, William, 79
Woodhull Lake, 79
Woodruff, Timothy, 107, 129
Woods and Waters, 17, 109, 116, 119, 122-124, 131
Wright, Jonathan, 45, 50
Yellowstone National Park, 129

About the Author

Philip G. Terrie fell in love with the Adirondacks while working at a camp on Long Lake in the 1960s. After graduating from Princeton he served as Assistant Curator for History at the Adirondack Museum. He earned a Ph.D. in American Studies from George Washington University and is now Professor of English and American Culture Studies at Bowling Green State University in Ohio. He is the author of *Forever Wild: Environmental Aesthetics and the Adirondack Forest Preserve* and many articles on Adirondack history in both scholarly and popular journals. He and his family spend their summers at a remote cabin on Long Lake.